The Scrawl of the Wild

WHAT PEOPLE
WRITE ON WALLS
—AND WHY

norton mockridge

The Scrawl of the Wild

WHAT PEOPLE WRITE ON WALLS —AND WHY

THE WORLD PUBLISHING COMPANY: CLEVELAND AND NEW YORK

Published by The World Publishing Company
2231 West 110th Street, Cleveland, Ohio 44102
Published simultaneously in Canada by
Nelson, Foster & Scott Ltd.

818.5
M

First Printing 1968

Library of Congress Catalog Card Number: 67–22915

Printed in the United States of America

Some of the examples of graffiti in this book
previously were published in the New York World
Journal Tribune and newspapers throughout the
country serviced by the United Feature Syndicate.

preface

THIS BOOK HAS BEEN BROUGHT TO YOU BY AN ESCALATOR.
If I hadn't been going up on the UP escalator in the Independent subway station at Fifty-third Street and Madison Avenue in Manhattan at 5:36 P.M. on September 2, 1966, and if Jay Nelson Tuck hadn't been going down on the DOWN escalator at 5:36 P.M. on September 2, 1966, you wouldn't be reading this book today.

But I *was* going up, and he *was* going down.

And in the few seconds that it took us to pass each other, *The Scrawl of the Wild* was conceived. And right out there in public, too!

I hadn't seen Jay Nelson Tuck for quite a few years—not since he and I had worked together in the early 1940s as rewrite men on the old *New York World-Telegram*. But he recognized me immediately, and I recognized him—even though he'd served a number of years as a TV critic and as an associate editor of *Medical World News*. (And that's *not* a non sequitur.)

We exchanged pleasantries—"My God! Norton Mockridge!" and "Well, I'll be damned! Jay Nelson Tuck!"—and then, as we noticed we were slipping away from each other (he going down, and I going up), we had that frustrating experience of wanting to say something to each other but not knowing what to say quickly enough before the other vanished.

Jay, however, kept his cool, even though sliding swiftly to the lower depths, and cried out:

"I've got something for you."

I, vanishing to somewhere up there, shouted:

"Great! What is it?"

Then I became conscious that quite a few people on the escalators, maybe fifty or more, were staring at me and I blushed. But even in that moment of extremity, I could hear Jay's voice, fading in the distance like a man falling down a well, crying:

"About graffiti . . . I'll write to you about it . . . I'll . . . write . . . to . . . you . . . tomorrow. . . ."

And then he was gone.

When I got home that night, I said to my wife:

"Ole Jay Nelson Tuck's gonna write to me tomorrow about graffiti."

"You must be out of your mind," she said. "Have you been drinking martinis?"

She said this because she never had heard of Jay Nelson Tuck and she never had heard of graffiti. And she knew through her woman's intuition that *I* never had heard of graffiti and most surely didn't know what it was. And she also knew that if I ever drink martinis, terrible things happen.

I explained to her that Jay Nelson Tuck was a friend I'd met on the escalator, that I hadn't had any martinis, and that we'd have to wait to find out what is graffiti. She seemed satisfied, and we each had a vodka and soda (a nasty drink, but not so fattening as vodka and tonic) and went out to dinner.

The next night when I got home, there, much to my surprise, was a letter from Jay Nelson Tuck. (The rapidity with which it got there shows that the Post Office Department can make mistakes when it wants to!) I ripped it open and discovered that Jay Nelson Tuck had been an avid reader of my daily newspaper column for some time and that he had been delighted with my columns on Fractured English, Backwards Language, Little Willies, Stinky Pinkies, City Bird Watching, and the funny little things that happen to all of us in everyday life.

But he severely took me to task for what he described as "a grave omission."

"Why," he asked, "have you ignored the rich, cultural, fascinating field of graffiti?"

I didn't know what the hell he was talking about. (Today, of course, everybody knows what is graffiti. But all of this was happening back in the dim, unenlightened age of 1966.) I went to my Webster's Third New International Dictionary, Unabridged (and, I hoped, unexpurgated), and looked up graffiti.

Well, I didn't see any *graffiti* right away, but I did find *graffito,* and I discovered that it sort of sifts down from such words as *graffio, graffiare, grafio,* and *graphium*—all of which, so far as I could make out, mean "to scratch." And then, much to my relief, my eye fell on *graffiti*—the plural of *graffito*. Lots of scratches.

The definition of *graffito* read: "An inscription, figure, or design scratched on rocks or walls or on artifacts made of plaster, stone, or clay. Compare *sgraffito*."

Big deal! I should write about scratchings on plaster, stone, or clay! Ha!

But, reading on in Jay's letter, I found that the art of graffiti is more than that. "We know it today," said Jay, "as the scrawlings by that great author, Anonymous, which appear on billposters, board fences, and walls, and especially the walls of washrooms."

"Possibly," said Jay, "you have been put off by the fact

that the vast bulk of this material is of little or no literary or sociological interest. Who cares, after all, whether 'Joe Loves Dottie,' except Joe? And—possibly—Dottie?

"But, buried within this mountain of chaff is much good, golden grain, waiting only to be sifted out. For example, a popular topic among graffiti authors at this time is the war in Viet Nam. And where will you find a more subversive slogan than this, which appears on a construction fence in Greenwich Village in New York: "Girl Scouts Wear the Green Beret"?

Jay went on and gave me many more examples of things he'd seen scribbled or lettered on walls, fences, posters, subway signs, vending machines, and other such places. And it was the first time I realized that the business of writing on walls had progressed beyond the four-letter words and the invectives such as "F—— You," "James Is a Fairy," and "Screw the World."

As I studied Jay's examples—and then later went on to look over thousands of other scrawls of the wild—it became apparent that a great deal of the finest, keenest, and most satirical and witty writing being done today is not necessarily in books, magazines, and newspapers—but on fences and walls! (One finds countless misspellings and grammatical errors, as you will see, but that doesn't seem to bother the folks who write graffiti.)

Let me give you a few samples right now. Some of them have been around a bit and you might well have heard them. But they're so good that they've become classic and thus bear repeating.

One of my favorites is this scribbling on a wall:

Death is Nature's Way of Telling You to Slow Down

And how about?:

Help a Nun Kick Her Habit

> *Don't Be a School Drop-Out.*
> *Stay in School and Drive the Teachers Nuts*

Or this variant:

> *Don't Be a School Drop-Out.*
> *Stay in School and Learn to Read and Riot*

Then there are such things as:

> *Support Mental Health or I'll Kill you*
>
> *Give Your Child Mental Blocks for Christmas*

You've seen those signs all across the country which read:

> *Jesus Saves*

Well, here are some of the things that have been written under "Jesus Saves":

> *Plaid Stamps*
>
> *But Moses Invests*
>
> *What For?*
>
> *He Couldn't Do It on My Salary!*

One of the great classics is this exchange found on a subway wall. Somebody had written:

> *My Mother Made Me a Homosexual*

Under which somebody else wrote in a very tiny script:

> *If I Get Her the Wool Will She Make Me*
> *One, Too?*

x

And then there was this interesting exchange. Some bitter character wrote:

Edith Sitwell Is a Transvestite

And under that, another observer of life scribbled:

She's Dead, Ya Dope

The first writer came back, read this and added:

Okay, Edith Sitwell Is a DEAD *Transvestite*

Such graffiti is so provocative that authors of books, plays, musicals, and TV shows often descend into the subways or prowl the construction fences to find lines and sometimes titles for their work.

Anthony Newley admits that he found the title *Stop the World, I Want to Get Off* written on a wall. Edward Albee picked up his mysterious title *Who's Afraid of Virginia Woolf?* by consulting a wall in the subway. And in another subway, my friend, author Robert Saffron, happily discovered the title of his book which Joseph Levine is making into a movie:

Is the U. S. Ready for Self-Government?

All right—enough of that. Now let's see how all this started, what it means, and why people do it.

I've studied it for many months now; I've consulted some experts and I've discussed it thoroughly with quite a few great brains—and I'm still not sure just what it's all about.

But it's tremendously fascinating, so let's see what we've got.

one

BACK IN 1,000,000 B.C., OR IT MIGHT HAVE BEEN A YEAR earlier, an anthropoid ape got tired of being an anthropoid ape and decided to become a Pithecanthropus erectus.

He didn't know it, of course, but he was the Adam of his Eolithic era and, like all Adams, he wanted a little female companionship.

So, he silver-tongued a female anthropoid ape into becoming a female Pithecanthropus erectus. He then ripped the beard off a dinosaur and made her a charming little miniskirt. She was so entrancing that he promptly fell in love with her.

And what was the first thing he did after that? I'll tell you what was the first thing he did.

He took his little eolith—which the dictionary tells us was "a crudely and irregularly chipped flint"—and strode over to the wall of his stone cave. Then, with a flourish and an adoring glance at his beloved, he made this inscription:

It took him something like twelve hours, during which time his spouse fell asleep. But when he had completed it, he was very proud of his handiwork and he awakened his mate to show it to her. She didn't know what it meant, because she couldn't read, of course, but he leaned over and whispered into her ear that it said:

Joe Loves Dottie

Then they parted the heavily matted hair that hung down over their faces, and they kissed.

This made them both very content, and they lived happily ever after—that is, until Joe met Sadie and fell in love with her because she was much younger than Dottie and, besides, she had less hair over her face. It was then that he returned to the wall, scratched out "Dottie," and wrote "Sadie" just above it.

All of this is interesting, and I'd like to take you through Joe's other conquests, but that would get us away from the point I'm trying to make.

My point is that Joe was the first human to indulge in graffiti!

I think he'd be proud of that, and even prouder to know

B.C.) got around to
ately known as "The
e Forum, the temple
Maximus.

grafficionados a mar-
rned out such joyous

_an_

l his day (550–478
g ("Man with Hole
" and so on). Xerxes
wrote all over the
nd Aristotle, Plato,
gs in public places,
nay, indeed, even be

en's room:

but how care-

Lesbos

out a thought that
today, he authored:

ism

attributed to him is:

Animal

that what he wrote is just about what kids are writing today. Of course, today there's more of the "Joe Loves Herman" kind of thing, but that needn't bother us in our historical study.

Anyway, Joe's eolithic writing, done as it was with a bit of flint, didn't last long and we have no samples of eolithic writing today. (I, in fact, am the only historian who even _knows_ that Joe wrote "Joe Loves Dottie.")

The next step in the history of graffiti came when, some 500,000 to 975,000 years later, characters like Java Man, Heidelberg Man, Peking Man, Neanderthal Man, and Cro-Magnon Man began using flaked stone tools and sharpened stone tools and spears.

Since these tools were stronger and sharper than the old pieces of flint, there were more "Joe Loves Dotties" chiseled all over cave walls than you could shake a stone hand axe at. And other expressions came into being.

There were such inscriptions as "Joe is a Fink," and "Dottie Loves Dottie," and "Who is Joe?" And some of the less morally inclined ladies took to lettering on mountains invitations like this one:

For Fun and Games, See Daphne. Cave No. 2

Then, as this earliest human culture got really swinging and invented stuff like pottery, on which you could jot a lot of graffiti, and good tin, copper, and cast-iron tools, a Golden Age of Graffiti began.

Hardly a rock or a wall or a tree was safe from random writing. And the literary lights of those days turned out some fine things, things that easily could compare with exciting quotations from such modern works as _Fanny Hill, Candy_, and _Valley of the Dolls_.

The art of graffiti had advanced to such a stage by 2775 B.C., for instance, that when the pyramids were built during the rule of the third to sixth dynasties in the Old

3

Kingdom of Egypt, the slaves who dragge[d]
heavy stone blocks frequently scratched on
timents as:

Workers of the World Unite!

Down With Slave Labor!

Join Local MMMMMCCCXXXXXIV

A friend of mine who visited the pyram[id]
ago inspected some of the old scratchings[,]
this message clearly imprinted:

Jimmy Hoffa Forever

There is, however, some possibility that t[hey]
been placed there in more recent years.

But there's plenty of authentic old-time g[raffiti]
samples of it that my researchers dug u[p]

Lucius Tarquinius Priscus (616–5[ ]
building the Cloaca Maxima (affect[ionately "The]
Great Sewer") and such things as [the temple]
of Jupiter Capitolinus, and the Cir[cus]

These wonderful surfaces gave t[hem a mar-]
velous opportunity and they quickly [added such]
quips as:

There's No Trustin' an Etru[scan]

Tar and Feather Tarquins

Lucius Loves Lucy

Lucius Is Luscious

Well, life went on—Confucius [(551–479]
B.C.) and scribbled all over everyt[hing such as]
in Pocket Easily Pull Down Underw[ear." Xerxes]
(519–465 B.C.) invaded Greece an[d wrote in one]
place: "Greek Restaurants Stink!"[Aeschylus]
and Sophocles all wrote little say[ings, too,]
some of which have been saved and [can still be]
read to this day.

Plato, for instance, scrawled in a[ ]

*Some say the Muses are nin[e—count them care-]
lessly!*
Look at the tenth, Sappho fr[om Lesbos.]

And once, thoughtlessly shootin[g off a line that]
would get him into *plenty* of troub[le:]

Democracy Passes into Desp[otism]

Aristotle was no better. A graffit[o of his:]

Man Is by Nature a Politica[l Animal]

that what he wrote is just about what kids are writing today. Of course, today there's more of the "Joe Loves Herman" kind of thing, but that needn't bother us in our historical study.

Anyway, Joe's eolithic writing, done as it was with a bit of flint, didn't last long and we have no samples of eolithic writing today. (I, in fact, am the only historian who even *knows* that Joe wrote "Joe Loves Dottie.")

The next step in the history of graffiti came when, some 500,000 to 975,000 years later, characters like Java Man, Heidelberg Man, Peking Man, Neanderthal Man, and Cro-Magnon Man began using flaked stone tools and sharpened stone tools and spears.

Since these tools were stronger and sharper than the old pieces of flint, there were more "Joe Loves Dotties" chiseled all over cave walls than you could shake a stone hand axe at. And other expressions came into being.

There were such inscriptions as "Joe is a Fink," and "Dottie Loves Dottie," and "Who is Joe?" And some of the less morally inclined ladies took to lettering on mountains invitations like this one:

For Fun and Games, See Daphne. Cave No. 2

Then, as this earliest human culture got really swinging and invented stuff like pottery, on which you could jot a lot of graffiti, and good tin, copper, and cast-iron tools, a Golden Age of Graffiti began.

Hardly a rock or a wall or a tree was safe from random writing. And the literary lights of those days turned out some fine things, things that easily could compare with exciting quotations from such modern works as *Fanny Hill, Candy,* and *Valley of the Dolls.*

The art of graffiti had advanced to such a stage by 2775 B.C., for instance, that when the pyramids were built during the rule of the third to sixth dynasties in the Old

3

Kingdom of Egypt, the slaves who dragged the incredibly heavy stone blocks frequently scratched on them such sentiments as:

Workers of the World Unite!

Down With Slave Labor!

Join Local MMMMMCCCXXXXXIV!

A friend of mine who visited the pyramids a few years ago inspected some of the old scratchings, and he found this message clearly imprinted:

Jimmy Hoffa Forever

There is, however, some possibility that that might have been placed there in more recent years.

But there's plenty of authentic old-time graffiti. The next samples of it that my researchers dug up were written

4

somewhere between 1900 and 1600 B.C., the first Babylonian dynasty.

It was then, you'll recall, that King Hammurabi placed all Mesopotamia under Babylonian power, instituted sweeping civil reform, and established the first systematic legal code. Everywhere, almost overnight, inscriptions like these appeared in public:

Hammurabi Go Home!

Baby Babylonia

Up Hammurabi!

Civil Service Workers Unite!

Along about 1350 B.C., when everybody got to working on the tomb of Pharaoh Tutankhamen, some sly and, I'm sorry to say, dirty-minded workmen scribbled some things on the wall that were so gamy that even the Hearst Sunday supplements didn't dare to publish them when the tomb was opened and inspected in 1922 D.H. and B.C. (during Harding and before Coolidge). Two that I like, of the less offensive group, however, are:

Pharaoh Schmaraoh!

For He's a Jolly Good Pharaoh!

And you should have seen what was written on the walls of King Solomon's temple in Jerusalem in the years between 947 and 932 B.C.! Scandalous! Really, the place should have been pulled down! I'll give you one of the lesser jibes:

Solomon Thinks He's a Wise Guy

Things were just as bad, however, by the time that

5

Lucius Tarquinius Priscus (616–578 B.C.) got around to building the Cloaca Maxima (affectionately known as "The Great Sewer") and such things as the Forum, the temple of Jupiter Capitolinus, and the Circus Maximus.

These wonderful surfaces gave the grafficionados a marvelous opportunity and they quickly turned out such joyous quips as:

> *There's No Trustin' an Etruscan*
>
> *Tar and Feather Tarquins*
>
> *Lucius Loves Lucy*
>
> *Lucius Is Luscious*

Well, life went on—Confucius had his day (550–478 B.C.) and scribbled all over everything ("Man with Hole in Pocket Easily Pull Down Underwear" and so on). Xerxes (519–465 B.C.) invaded Greece and wrote all over the place: "Greek Restaurants Stink!" And Aristotle, Plato, and Sophocles all wrote little sayings in public places, some of which have been saved and may, indeed, even be read to this day.

Plato, for instance, scrawled in a men's room:

> *Some say the Muses are nine, but how carelessly!*
> *Look at the tenth, Sappho from Lesbos*

And once, thoughtlessly shooting out a thought that would get him into *plenty* of trouble today, he authored:

> *Democracy Passes into Despotism*

Aristotle was no better. A graffito attributed to him is:

> *Man Is by Nature a Political Animal*

6

And Sophocles, so they say, chalked out:

For Money You Would Sell Your Soul

A Woman Should Be Seen, Not Heard

War Never Slays a Bad Man in Its Course,
but the Good Always!

Of course, I can't prove that these men wrote these things. Maybe they had their Bacons or Boswells, but I do know that the public generally accepted these graffiti as the products of their minds.

Now in the years between 468 and 399 B.C., Socrates, as you know, got crosswise with the Athenian state and was accused of corrupting the young. And everywhere you went in those days you'd see scrawled on the walls:

Sock Socrates

Socrates Hates Hippies

Then, after he was condemned to death and made to drink the lethal potion, hundreds of people wrote:

Beware of No-Cal Hemlock

Alexander the Great (immortalized musical graffito: "Alexander's Ragtime Band"), the Ptolemies—I, II, III, IV, V, VI, VII, VIII, and IX—and Hannibal, Caesar, Cleopatra, and Caligula all came in for their share of graffiti.

There's no need to repeat any of it here, but an example of graffiti involving Caesar and Cleopatra is well worth mention. It was lettered in all the public baths and it read:

If Cleopatra Sits upon Her Asp, Will Julius
Caes-her?

7

So it went. Kings and queens fought, countries went to war, people starved, church and state locked in bitter battles, Charlemagne invented champagne, the Crusades were held, Macbeth gave it to Duncan, the Magna Carta was written, and Genghis Khan and Henry VIII had their fun—just to name a few things that inspired people to produce a bundle of graffiti.

Henry VIII, to be sure, might well not be remembered today had it not been for graffiti, especially for one generally credited to Cardinal Wolsey (or maybe it was Sir Thomas More), which read:

> *Ladies—Pray Do Not Lose Your Heads over*
> *Henry*

People went on and on, writing on walls, and when Columbus reached America in 1492, he went to a cute little inn in the Bahamas, ordered a tankard of rum, and repaired to the men's room while it was being served. There upon the wall, much to his astonishment, he found lettered:

Leif Ericsson Was Here

He was distressed, of course, especially because the graffito bore the date "1000," but he was even more distressed when he sailed on to Cuba and found this notation:

Leif Ericsson Was Here

TWICE!

This grieved Columbus, and it didn't help Queen Isabella's digestion much, either. But I should like to point out that Ericsson himself had been just as grieved 492 years earlier. Landing that year, 1000, on the North American coast, Leif also went to a men's room (it had been a long voyage), and there in bold letters upon the wall he found:

Kilroy Was Here

Kilroy, as you're aware, was the greatest explorer of them all, and, furthermore, he's lasted through the ages. I guess there isn't anywhere he hasn't been, and he certainly never has been without pencil or pen. Only recently, social arbiter Amy Vanderbilt came to me excitedly and said:

"I've just returned from a trip to Italy and I want to tell you that in the men's room in Dante's Tomb in Ravenna there is written on the wall: 'Kilroy Was Queer.'"

I didn't ask Amy how come she'd noted this inscription in the *men's* room, and she didn't volunteer any explanation. But I know that when Amy says a thing is so, *it is so.*

There's no need, I suspect, to go on and tell you how all down through history the graffiti writers have done their bit. They were there, bravely carrying on, when Americans, masquerading as Indians, tossed all that British tea into Boston Harbor in 1773. Right away the Boston waterfront was decorated with glowing words like:

Take Tea and Sea

Lipton Go Home

Up Your Tetley

The Indians Get Shafted Again!

And the men who caused to be engraved in the annals of history such expressions as "Give me liberty, or give me death," "Don't tread on me," and "Don't fire until you see the whites of their eyes," obviously found them first, as Newley, Albee, and Saffron found *their* best lines, upon the walls of various publick houses.

Such is the graffiti writers' contribution to history and to letters.

But who is writing graffiti today—what are they writing —and why?

two

THE STUDY OF THE ART OF GRAFFITI IS ENORMOUSLY COM-
plicated because nobody, apparently, knows the people who
write it. I never have met a man or woman who admits
that he or she has written, is writing, or ever will write
upon walls. But *somebody* does it!

I know of only one instance where a graffiti writer was
observed. It seems that a young man named H. G. Mc-
Lean, Jr., a journalism student at New York University,
was standing in the West Fourth Street station of the IND
Subway on the afternoon of May 3, 1967 (oh, historic
date!), when a small, bald man in his late fifties walked
up to an ice-cream vending machine and pulled out a
black marking pencil.

McLean, who later reported the whole ghastly incident
to me, noted that the man was wearing a seedy topcoat
that was half-covered with campaign-type buttons. Some
of the buttons read: "Save Water. Shower With a Friend,"
"It's Not the Work That Gets Me Down, It's the Coffee
Breaks," "Draft Beer—Not Students," and "Pray for Sex."

As McLean watched, the man wrote on the machine:
"Make Love, and If You Want to Make War, Enjoy Your-
self." Then he wrote: "God is Dead" and "I Am a Cunning
Linguist."

McLean walked over and asked the man why he was
writing these things.

11

"Can't ya read, mister?" snarled the little man.

"Yes," said McLean, "but *why* do you write these things in public places?"

At this, McLean told me, the man blanched and spat at him, then turned and ran out of the station as though being chased by a pack of wild animals.

Well, that was quite an experience, and I submit that, as a result of it, H. G. McLean, Jr., journalism student, is a fortunate human indeed—a man set apart. He is, so far as I know, the only man in the world who has watched a writer of graffiti in action.

People just don't see these mysterious poets, lyricists, satirists, and scatological scribblers when they create.

Whoever saw anybody write "Kilroy Was Here?" Yet—it has appeared in millions of places. And billions of other words, expressions, sentences, and bits of poetry and prose are being written every year on our fences, walls, sidewalks, ad posters, pavements, and telephone booths. For the last year I've asked everybody I know:

"Did you ever write anything in a public place?"

And to a man, they've said, "No."

But damn it, *somebody* writes it, and they cleverly pick a time when nobody is looking. Again, I congratulate Mc-Lean on having caught one in the act. The only other person I know who even came close to catching a graffitist at work is my old army buddy, Major Fred Pool, now the executive director of the Eastern Texas Chamber of Commerce.

Fred was just about to enter a public toilet in Longview, Texas, when a man he knew came out. And this man *was putting a pencil back into his shirt pocket.*

Fred was shocked, for this man was one of the town's best-educated and most respected citizens.

"Good Lord," cried Fred, staring at the man, "I never dreamed that you engage in scribbling on the walls of our public toilets."

The man gave Fred a cold, withering glance.

"I really don't, of course," he said. "I was *just* correcting some English, that's all."

Be that as it may—there simply isn't any place that's safe from graffiti. I've seen it in churches, in the Senators' washroom in Washington, in a nunnery (maybe Amy Vanderbilt will ask *me* how I got there!), on tombstones, on

13

the Washington Monument, in a Christian Science reading room, and in a corridor in the American Bible Society building.

Only a few years ago, the Statue of Liberty was the most graffitied-up place in the world. It seemed as though at least half of the many millions of visitors to the revered monument had written their names, addresses, ages, loves, sexual preferences, telephone numbers, and political observations and other acid thoughts on the figure, both inside and out.

They had used pen, pencil, lipstick, crayon, chalk, and pocketknives. Inside the main entrance, leading to the elevator, the walls were completely covered with this kind of doodling. Some of the inscriptions were:

Liberty Is a Lousy Trip

Liberty Stinks

Who Needs Liberty?

The French Screwed Us

Liberty Go Home!

That area, however, was a pale nothing compared with the artwork inside the elevator that goes to the upper platform, and on the walls throughout the 168-step ascent. The walls at first glance seemed to be an almost continuous lipstick mural.

Most of the lipstickmanship was in the "May Loves John," "Jack, Ted, and Willie—Seeing the Sights," and "Mr. and Mrs. Mickey Marasco, Gopher Gulch, Nev., 1935" class.

But there were hundreds of thousands of others, including:

Bring Back Al Capone

14

Eleanor Roosevelt Plays Squat Tag on the Lawn

If You Want Liberty—or Anything Else— Call Percy, TR 9-0000 (Girls Don't Bother to Call)

Liberty Is Pregnant!

And under that one, somebody had written:

Call Dr. Schwartz, CI 6-0000. He Helped Me Out

The amazing thing in connection with much of this inside graffiti, however, was how it got on the walls. Visitors had to climb out on steel girders to reach the walls, which were six feet or more from the spiral staircase. The fact that the graffiti artists risked a five-story fall apparently didn't bother them at all.

In time, things got so bad that Charles S. Marshall, superintendent of the monument, ordered a vast cleaning job and expunged all of the graffiti. Then, to keep the Lady clean, he installed a woven wire guard between the wall and the staircase, and the walls at the bottom of the monument were given a coat of lipstick-proof paint.

But still, the scribbling went on wherever anybody could wield a pen or a knife. Said the superintendent:

"They'd carve on the torch if they could crawl up there."

Libraries are great places to find graffiti. In the main branch of the New York Public Library are these literary adornments:

Judge Crater Is Hiding Behind the Sex Books

Occupancy by More Than 489 Persons Is Dangerous, Unlawful, and Damn Unsanitary

15

Legalize Cancer

Millard Fillmore Was a Dirty Commie Rat

Librarians Are Lesbians

God Is Retrogressive and Hostile

How You Gonna Keep 'Em Down on the Farm, After They've Seen Parity?

Old Soldiers Never Die—Just Young Ones

Books Give You Syphilis

In the Yale Library:

Support Free Enterprise—Legalize Prostitution

Reagan Only Wants to Use the White House as a Stepping Stone

Chastity Is Its Own Punishment

God Isn't Dead—He Just Doesn't Want to Get Involved

Chicken Little Was Right

The Literary Digest Lives!

And in the Princeton Library:

Caning Is a Punishment for Young Boys—A Sport for Young Men

Gov. Romney—Deep, Deep Down He Is Shallow

I Can Resist Anything but Temptation

At Cornell:

16

Studying Causes Cancer

Wear Contraceptives. The Unborn Will Bless You

If You Liked Hitler, You'll Love Lyndon

On campuses all over the country, as well as on city fences, where people had written references to God, such as:

God Is Dead—Nietzsche

Nietzsche Is Dead—God

there appeared a new phrase when Senator Thomas Dodd got into the jam that led to his censure. Almost overnight, these words were printed, scribbled, and penciled everywhere:

Dodd Is Dead

How that spread so swiftly across the country, nobody knows. But spread it did.

Another thing that's spread quickly of late is the "Overby" kick. This is something like Kilroy but, whereas Kilroy never did anything but announce he "was here," Overby takes lots of actions and expresses lots of thoughts. Examples:

Overby Rules

Overby Never Died

Overby Is Living with Hitler and God in Argentina

Draft Me and Overby Will Overkill

Overby Burned My Draft Card

Overby Has a Heskinny in His Frebus

Overby Smokes Bananas

Overby Says Hugh Hefner Is a Virgin

Overby Will Deliver Us from McNamara

Overby Go Home!

Whether Overby ever will become as popular as Kilroy is uncertain, but at the moment he's making quite a splash. Now, let's see why people are writing all this stuff.

three

WHO WRITES GRAFFITI? AND WHY?

Well, the who is the easier question.

Apparently, people of all ages, of both sexes, of two or three other sexes, of all nationalities, and of every station in life, from the lowest clod to some of our top sophisticates and intellectuals, indulge in the practice of writing on walls at one time or other.

This is deduced from extensive studies of graffiti made by folklore experts and other authorities, and by medical men and professors who have explored various aspects of this mysterious practice. And I'll tell you about some of their findings later on.

But why do these people write graffiti? And, having written it, why are they ashamed to admit it?

There are, to be sure, some wall scribblers who proudly sign their names to their work, along with addresses, telephone numbers, dimensions, and preferences. But they are an extremely small minority, and almost all of them are gay boys who are eager to make contacts.

I have talked to more than a score of psychiatrists, psychologists, graphologists, folklore researchers, professors, and educators, and I must tell you right away quickly —these learned people are anything but positive about what the reasons are.

Oh, they've formed opinions, and they've guessed a bit,

and they've applied the fundamental rules of psychiatry and psychology to the problem, but they've come up with a lot of different answers.

Kinsey, in his *Sexual Behavior in the Human Female*, dipped fairly deeply into this puzzler under the headings of: "Erotic Writing and Drawing" and "Wall Inscriptions" but he, of course, dealt with the sexual and pornographic graffiti exclusively and never touched on the political, the humorous, the philosophical, and so on.

However, I believe that much of what he said about motivation can be applied in large measure to all writers of graffiti. In general, he said that his studies indicated that the writing on the wall is intended for self-stimulation and for the stimulation of others. This is particularly true, it would seem, of things applying to sex. But it no doubt has the same effect, or is intended to have the same effect, in, let's say, the political field, the field of foreign relations, or the problem of war.

How about these put-downs of the Viet Nam War?:

The Viet Cong Are the Good Guys

War Is Good Business—Invest Your Sons

Take a Viet Cong to Lunch This Week

Viet Nam: The Edsel of Foreign Policy

Lock Up McNamara and Throw Away the Ky

Those little billet-doux ought to stimulate just about everybody, and particularly the guys who wrote them.

Kinsey declares that most toilet wall inscriptions "provide information on the extent and the nature of the suppressed sexual desires of females and males.

"The inscriptions most frequently deal with activities which occur less frequently in the actual histories [of the writers]. This means that the males who make the inscriptions, and the males who read them, are exposing their unsatisfied desires. The inscriptions portray what they would like to experience in real life.

"Usually, the inscriptions are anonymous. They are usually located in restricted, hidden, or remote places. Most of the males who make them would not so openly express their erotic interests in places where they could be identified."

Kinsey found, interestingly enough, that females do very little of the scrawling on walls—that is, beyond the puppy-love, teeny-bopper scribbles of the "Mary Loves Matty" variety. And he found that when females write on walls in toilets, only 25 per cent of that material is sexual. But male writing in toilets is 86 per cent sexual. And much of that deals with perversion.

Typical of the kind of material found in a ladies' john are these:

Minnie Mouse Is a Jew

The Name of the Pill Is Absorbine Jr.

Give Ethel the Pill

'Tis Better to Have Loved an Hermaphrodite Than Never to Have Loved at All

21

But most of the jottings in the men's toilets are pretty strong:

Sodomy Is a Summer Festival

Thou Shalt Not Covet Thy Neighbor's Fag

Sex Is a Dirty Habit, But It's Easily Overcome

Underneath which was written in a different hand:

Hell, I'd Rather Give Up Eatin'

I've Got What Every Woman Wants

Below which was written:

Then You Must Be in the Fur Business

Merry Syphilis and Happy Gonorrhea

Now Being Organized: The Greenwich Village Heterosexual Club

Use Contraceptives—Take the Worry Out of Being Close

Nobody Loves You When You're Old and Gay

*Young Man with Beautiful Body—Willing to Do Anything—*PS, *If You See This, Bill, Don't Bother to Call. It's Only Me, Tony*

The Penis Mightier Than the Sword

Kinsey points out that most of the inscriptions and drawings in men's rooms have to do with male organs and male functions, and that very few have to do with female organs and functions. This, it is believed, indicates that they are the work of homosexuals or males who are unusually interested in male organs and functions. Personally, I think that many of them are copied from doodles that Benjamin Franklin made while he was editing *Poor Richard's Almanack,* but that, of course, is just an opinion.

In any case, Kinsey says that the male usually derives erotic satisfaction out of his writing and drawings "and he may derive even greater satisfaction in anticipating that the inscriptions he makes will arouse other males, amounting sometimes to hundreds and thousands of other males who may subsequently see them."

Incidentally, this reminds me that many of the researchers and other experts with whom I consulted frequently lamented the fact that even though it's written abundantly, graffiti, unfortunately, generally has a rather short life.

"Just think of the thousands, perhaps millions, of brilliant and witty things that have been written on walls," said one researcher, "only to be washed away by stupid cleaning men and women. God, I wish there could be some way to preserve them."

Along this line, let me tell you about what happened in Chumley's Restaurant, 86 Bedford Street, in Greenwich Village. For many years, this restaurant was a magnificent source of graffiti for the advanced collector, and the walls of the washrooms and of the dining area itself became black with writing—much of it hilarious, if unprintable.

One day some patron, apparently irked by all the writing on the walls, took a huge Magic Marker pen and wrote on one wall in enormous letters:

Down With Graffiti!

And the next day, under that, somebody wrote:

Yeah. Down With All Wops

Well, the owner of the restaurant, Ray Santini, got a big laugh out of the exchange. But then, even though he himself is of Italian origin, he got to worrying that some customer of Italian extraction might be offended. And besides, he'd grown more than a little tired of all the graffiti.

So, one night he brought in a crew and had all walls and ceilings painted. Not a single graffito was left. Santini was pleased with the freshness of the place—until he went into the restaurant one morning and found that someone had scrawled in bold letters on one of the clean walls:

SANTINI IS A BOOK BURNER!!!

Two psychiatrists I talked with disagreed with Kinsey to some extent. They didn't feel that most of the wall writing is a result of unsatisfied or suppressed desires, indicative of what the writer would like to experience in real life.

They contended that the writers are little more than exhibitionists, not too far advanced from childhood.

"Every child, or surely *almost* every child," said one of these skull feelers, "writes or draws or scribbles on walls. From the time they can creep and get hold of a pencil or crayon, children will mark up anything they can reach. This is only natural, a normal desire to show the world what the child can do, how talented it is.

"When the child gets older, he realizes that writing on walls is an infantile practice at best, and he finds other methods of displaying his thoughts and his talent—writing on blackboards and paper, drawing sketches and making fingerpaintings, and so on. But, as you know, many children never really grow up. It's my personal opinion that much of the graffiti is written by these anxiety-ridden adolescents."

The other dissenting psychiatrist took this tack, too, but went beyond it. He felt that two major emotions are largely responsible: the striving for omnipotence, and anti-social feelings.

In the first category you have such graffiti as:

Black Power over All

The Green Hornets Is Best

25

Jimmy Is King

Harry's Good for Four a Night. Ask Jayne

I'm 10 Inches Long and Three Inches Around

Under which some wag wrote:

Crazy Man! But How Long Is Your P——?

In the second category, anti-social feelings, you have:

F—— You!

Peter Is a Pansy

Burn All Niggers

Be a Man, Join the Klan

All Whites Are Bastards and Sick, Sick, Sick

The Great Society Is a Cesspool

Mayor Lindsay Was a Test Tube Baby

Writer Warren Boroson, in *Fact* magazine, indicates, however, that much of the graffiti being written today is merely a result of the desire of people of all classes to express themselves, openly and freely, albeit anonymously.

"In poverty-stricken areas," he says, "the man lying in the street has few literary outlets for his hot-blooded polemics, and hence uses chalk and the nearest wall to express his discontent." He cited "Yanqui Go Home" in South America, and "I Hate Mr. Skins," in Watts, as typical examples.

Graffiti, he said, is having a glorious rebirth. "Once despised and sneered at by all save students of psychopathology," he wrote, "today graffiti are being searched out and scrutinized by journalists, politicians, sociologists, and even by ordinary men and women who happen to appreciate wit and whimsy."

Boroson points out, too, that in totalitarian countries, "the graffito is the last, all-but-ineradicable medium of free speech." For, he says, "even if 1984 does come to pass, in the dead of night a malcontent can always slip out and scrawl on a sidewalk: 'Down With Big Brother!'"

And he declares that irrefutable evidence of the new fascination with graffiti lies in the way newspapers and magazines have been quoting them as expressions of popular opinion.

He also points out that the Sexual Revolution—with its greater freedoms, lifting of taboos, and open discussions of the most intimate physical relationships—is responsible for the resurgence of witty graffiti.

Characters who used to get their kicks from writing four-letter words on walls, words which now can be found in books, magazines, and other media, and which are heard from stage and screen, have had to turn to something else. As a result, he says, deviates have largely ceased writing obscenities on subway walls and have turned to expressing sentiments such as: "Bomb Hanoi."

"This, by Gresham's Law," says Boroson, "has left the field open to the wits, and the result is that some of the cleverest writing in America today can be found scrawled on walls . . . and the future promises more of the same. As totalitarianism increases, we can expect to see ever more political graffiti. And as the Sexual Revolution inches ahead, we can look forward to a profusion of witty graffiti. Clearly, the handwriting is on the wall."

Some of the handwriting he cites is this:

Marvin Can't Relate to His Environment ·

Support Mental Health Like Crazy

The Lord Giveth and the Lord Taketh Away;
Indian-Giver Be the Name of the Lord.

27

James Baldwin Eats Watermelon

Screw Home Cooking

And this exchange:

I Love Grils

This was crossed out and underneath was written:

I Love Girls

And the next day, in a new handwriting, was:

What About Us Grils?

four

ONE OF THE PSYCHIATRISTS WITH WHOM I DISCUSSED GRAF-fiti took the position that virtually all of it is written by emotionally unbalanced people who are seeking release from pressure.

"These people," he said, "undoubtedly suffer from a wide range of neuroses and psychoses. They are unable to properly adjust to their environment and they cannot stand the demands of what is described as everyday, normal society.

"This, of course, builds tremendous tension and anxiety and a release must be obtained. Some of the people so afflicted achieve at least a partial release by fighting with their wives or husbands, some by excessive drinking, some by staging temper tantrums, some by being destructive—like smashing dishes and glasses, kicking things over, hurling stones through windows, and setting fire to things.

"The man who writes graffiti—if, indeed, that is all he does to effect the release—is, to be sure, the least dangerous and bothersome of the psychotics. Most assuredly, there should be no movement to hinder him in this therapeutic pursuit. In fact, I believe he should be encouraged."

The doctor cited several examples of how troubled men have dissipated their hostilities by taking crayon in hand. I'll give you just one case which, I think, will be enough to give you the idea.

"This case," said the doctor, "was a man in his fifties.

Successful in business, liked by his associates and tolerated by his children—a man who, as you can see, was better off than most of us—he nonetheless sometimes fell into traumatic pseudocatatonia, which, as you know, is a catatonic state that might well follow a severe injury.

"However, I ascertained that he *had not* been physically injured; he merely had come into *prolonged conflict* with his mother-in-law.

"Well, after several consultations, I advised him to write his thoughts about his mother-in-law on paper, thus to get them out into the open, so to speak, and perhaps to permit them to evaporate to the winds. That was what I suggested, but after he'd filled nearly a thousand sheets of paper with his thoughts about his mother-in-law, he went a bit further than that.

"One day he took a bucket of white paint and a paint brush and on a red brick wall across the street from the window of his mother-in-law's sitting room, he laboriously painted in letters four feet high:

"After that he slept well nights, stopped snarling at his wife and children, devoted the proper attention to business and, in fact, was able to sit through entire meals without hearing any of the mother-in-law's caustic criticism that once threatened to drive him totally insane."

Other psychiatrists agreed with this reasoning and treatment, at least in part, but one eminent gentleman who has gained national honors for his skill in dealing with disorders of the psyche, refused to go along with the sober thoughts expressed by his colleagues.

This doctor, who has published two distinguished papers on human behavior and currently is engaged in writing a book that represents an attempt to extend Darwin's theories of evolution to human behavior, told me quite frankly that "to do a deadly scientific analysis of graffiti is incongruity beyond my comprehension."

He therefore delivered himself of the following paper:

31

"To begin with, in this short dissertation on the scientific principles, origins, history, methodology, and psychological motivation underlying the phenomena, I *reject* all extant theories 'explaining graffiti. Such theories are little more than a whimsical prejudice of their originators.

"The theories being manifold, I can, at best, demolish only a few by way of illustration:

"First, the untenable 'love theory,' based on an analysis of the 'John Loves Mary' form. The theorist here makes the error that the graffiti were set down by one John (or Mary), when closer study reveals that in ninety-four per cent of the cases, the graffiti were authored by individuals who hated John, Mary, or both.

"Second, the 'outhouse or pay-toilet' theory. This theory states that graffiti are organically related by associated cognitive processes to excretory functions, etc., etc. This is absurd. The theorist here confuses the underlying conditions for creativity with a geographical or special setting which provides: one, solitude for meditative thought; two, space to write, and three, 'captive' readers.

"Third, 'the Freudian view,' often referred to by cognoscenti as 'the Dingle-Berry Theory.' (Dingle-Berry is the scientific term for penis.)

"This theory simply asserts that every little boy wants to kill (and possibly eat) his father, following which repast, as Jones has so graphically represented, castration terror or no, the boy wishes to loll around in sexual dalliance with his mother, or proxies thereof.

("I refer, to be sure, to *Tom* Jones, not Ernest, whose biography of Freud remains the standard work.)

"The fact, of course, is that Freud—along with millions of other little boys—was undoubtedly scared green, not of his father, but of his mother, and would probably have clung tightly to his father except that his father seldom was home, or if home, was timid or preoccupied.

"The threat to the boy's Dingle-Berry as a source of

inspiration for graffiti turns out to be nothing more than a mote in Freud's eye. Dingle-Berry references constitute a trivial percentage of present-day graffiti; preoccupation with one's Dingle-Berry, in short, turns out to be a fad.

"As for the larger subject of sex itself, this too, is secondary, related simply to its being a fertile source of humor. As the great philosopher Immanuel Kant pointed out centuries ago, if you ponder on it a bit, sexual intercourse becomes ridiculously comical!

"The fact is that graffiti is quite adequately explained by reference to Newton's Law. I refer, of course, not to Isaac Newton, but to Mrs. Euphrosyne Newton of Brooklyn, a lady who for some years was a patient of a colleague of mine.

"Mrs. Newton was married to a heavy-set, muscular man, deeply involved in a program of physical fitness, who kept himself in tip-top shape by punching his wife around. To justify this, he explained to her that she talked too much, although she actually was a woman of few words.

"She once said to her husband: 'You can't stop me from thinking,' following which he knocked out her teeth, and following which my colleague proclaimed her remark to be Newton's Law—since which time it has remained unshakable, at least to my colleague and myself.

"Now, as the H-bomb is nothing more than a quite harmless extension of Einsteinian Relativity, so also is graffiti nothing more than an extension of Newton's Law. That there have been, of course, minor refinements in the practical application of the law goes without saying; exponents and practitioners of graffiti, unlike Mrs. Newton, often have their teeth.

"I hope I have made clear at this point my disdain for so-called scholars who have concocted histories of graffiti consisting of one small part scholarship, and ninety-nine parts fabrication derived from patent motives of self-aggrandizement.

"Newton's Law clearly shows the falsity of tracing graffiti back through history to Pompeii, long buried under volcanic ash (evidence that they possessed the H-bomb is absurd). Graffiti must be traced back to total silence—'*You can't stop me from thinking!*'

"And it is at this point where most of us still are, womb-entombed, unborn, our talent for graffiti unexplored, unrevealed, but showing by our silent reading proof of membership in the graffiti fraternity of Mankind.

"What's more—as an earlier statement of mine on the subject clearly demonstrates—graffiti did not spring full blown from the head of Zeus—a curse upon false myth-makers—but it is subject to that slow development characteristic of all organic evolution.

"The first graffiti were only one step removed from total silence, nothing but inaudible mumblings transcribed on available surfaces, and as untranslatable as chicken tracks in the snow. It becomes clear that in their proto-form, far from being either proclamations or even assertions, they

34

were essentially cabalistic signs, purposely unintelligible (as today's Maffiti or Mafia might make its secret sign in chalk on the cornerstone of Gracie Mansion).

"It was from such a common trunk that graffiti developed and evolved toward its present status as Everyman's Editorial. It was I, working deep in a cave lit by a flickering torch, who made the first stone rubbings which, translated from the Runic as KWH, we all recognize today as 'Kilroy Was Here.'

"True, the Grafia-Mafia bond was never totally severed. This was, in fact, the reason I eschewed full Grafia membership. Years ago, before I had ascended the scholarship ladder to the upper rungs, I made what I thought was a gentle bid for membership.

"Somewhat put off by typical samples of graffiti that I encountered in the men's room at the race track (Belmont, as I recall), I scrawled as a gentle remonstrance:

You Write Graffiti; Winners Write History

"The following day, returning at my usual time, I found scrawled beneath my statement the following rejoinder, embittered, no doubt, due to a speech impediment:

The P-P-Paths of W-W-Winners L-L-Lead
but to the W-W-Win-Window

"A fine 'in' joke, I mused cynically, and I decided if you can't join 'em, study 'em. That I have done, a long and intricate undertaking ending with truth and mellowness derived from true bigness.

"Grafia, unlike Mafia, have given up secret handshakes, codes, and such things. But a momentary exchange of glances as two members of the sect meet, conveys the tripartite message of the world-wide fraternity of graffiti:

35

Keep Out of Stir

Get Your Message in Print

Grab a Little Sex, One Way or the Other

"The warning is clear. The individual with a wipe of **Mr.** Clean who expunges even the lowliest example of graffiti from halls, walls, or stalls may continue to do so.

"*However*—he no longer can do so with impunity! He is violating Newton's Law and the gravity of it!"

five

RICHARD FREEMAN, WHO WROTE A BOOK CALLED *Graffiti* which was published in England by Hutchinson, declares: "Broadly speaking, writing a graffito is an aggressive act, and therefore a satisfying one. In two ways.

"First," he says, "the author is getting something off his mind. Second, the actual defacement, preceded by a feeling of tension, is the sexual act writ small. If you don't believe this, try it.

"A graffito does also give you an idea of participation. Ground crews write messages on bombs they cannot drop themselves. Girls write adoring messages on the vans pop groups use to tour the country. Tourists secure for themselves an inch of immortality by putting their names on the wall of a national monument."

Freeman and his partner, Tony Evershed, explored a great deal of London to find the graffiti for their book. "To make the collection," he writes, "we spent a lot of pennies, drank in a large number of pubs (not necessarily in that order), hopped on and off underground trains, and walked miles and miles."

The author says that good graffiti is hard to find and he wonders why some surfaces are never touched and others become crammed with scrawls. "A virgin whitewashed wall in a pub lavatory," he declares, "will go unspoilt for a year or two. Then one graffito appears, and the spell is broken. Writings spread over it like a rash."

A few examples that Freeman gives are:

A man's ambition must be small—
Who writes upon a s——house wall

Practice Birth Control—People Are Worse
Than the Bomb

The Worst Englishman Is the Englishman
Who Thinks and Acts Like One
                    (signed) *Confucius*

Mr. Wilson Make Hash and Rape Legal

I kiss them, I court them, I lie by their side,
And when I am tired I get up and ride

In common with most students of graffiti, Freeman is surprised that hardly anybody ever sees a wall writer at work. He interviewed a number of people in places where examples were in great profusion, but nobody had seen them written.

"In fifteen years on the beat," said a policeman to Freeman, "I've never yet caught anyone at it." And the manager of a Knightsbridge pub is quoted as saying:

"It's uncanny. As though they were written by an invisible man. I'm always popping down to the cellar here, and always glance into the gents as I go past, and I've never seen anyone writing on the wall. Ten years I've been here."

Freeman says he can understand how somebody could scribble something quickly and be undetected, but what worries him is how people find time to execute—unobserved —some of the more elaborate, detailed drawings that are found in public places, such as subway and railroad stations.

"I should think station personnel have a go at it themselves," he says. "The cleaners and platform staff are the only people who get enough privacy to turn a poster advertising a Russian ballet company dancing the Sleeping Beauty on film into a phallus-packed danse macabre."

One of the most remarkable pieces of graffiti I've ever

heard of is one that Freeman and Evershed found on the wall of a closet in one of the Middlesex hockey clubs.

It consisted of one sentence, "Wash off with soap and water," written eighty-two times in this fashion:

Wash off with soap and water
Wash off with soap and water
Wash off with soap and water
Wash off with soap and water
Wash off with soap and water

"A girl wrote these," says Freeman, "and there are two interpretations. Either her conscience told her to write it out so many times because of an act (sexual?) or incident which had disturbed her, so that she was 'doing lines' like any schoolgirl. Or it's a kind of nihilistic joke, and instead of meaning 'Wash (it) off with soap and water' the sense is 'Wash (this) off with soap and water.'"

Another serious student of graffiti is Robert Reisner, scholar, music critic, and nightclub owner, who wrote *Selected Scrawls from Bathroom Walls,* published by Parallax. Reisner, with whom I appeared on the David Susskind TV show when part of it was devoted to graffiti, concentrated on the writing in men's and women's toilets. He told me that in his exploration he washed his hands at least fifty times a day.

While he is happy with what he found, he weeps for what he didn't find.

"Washing my hands in countless lavatories in the course of my research," he said, "I was saddened by the thought that a vast fund of original humor is being washed away by zealous cleaning people every day.

"We should establish a society of serious scholars and give them the funds so that field trips can be made into the toilets of the world. Who knows what precious quips may be found in the pissoirs of Paris or the water closets of the Watusi?"

Reisner dug up a graffiti analyst who told him:

"Wall inscriptions are usually written by men who don't have the courage to have sex. A lot of the writings in women's toilets are done by men who sneak into them. Some were found to be the work of janitors and custodians."

One of the most interesting things that Reisner discovered is that the most virulent hate messages are found in places where it is common to see white women with Negro men and Negro women with white men.

He found that "there was an atmosphere of great camaraderie among the mixed patrons," but it was in sharp contrast to the hate messages in the rest rooms. "The comments," he noted, "probably are the true feelings which the writer dare not express among the people with whom he associates."

He found such writings as:

Burn, Baby, Burn

You People Are Sick, White Bastards
(signed) *An Indian*

Whitey Has Had It Baby

Why Try to Blot It Out?

41

Underneath which was written:

Face It. Blacky Is Not too Bright!

I talked to several graphologists to see whether they could analyze the writers of graffiti and they agreed that in general the writing on walls is nearly as indicative of characteristics as is handwriting on paper.

"The wall scribbler," said Dorothy Sara, a New York handwriting analyst, "usually does not follow his ordinary cursive script handwriting. He becomes a printer. He does not write in his usual size of script, but usually he writes (or prints) in much larger formations.

"The printing and the enlarged size of the graffito show the creative urge and the desire to project his (or her) personality far beyond his real capacity to do so.

"The scribbler makes a strong bid for attention, for flattery that will feed his ego."

Some examples of this are:

Robert! The One and Onlis!

My Name Is George D. I Steal

*I Am the Rightful Heir to President Poke,
but Nobody Will Listen to Me.*

I Is a Pervert

With this written below:

Yes You Is

The New Yorker magazine, which for years has been interested in graffiti and published some samples of it, ran a cartoon some years ago, which is illustrative of this ego-flattery kind of wall scrawl. The sketch shows a kid with

42

a paint pot and brush in his hand standing in front of a brick wall on which he has painted:

Shari Loves Frankie
Barbara Loves Frankie
Penny Loves Frankie
Alice Loves Frankie
Pat Loves Frankie
Marcia Loves Frankie
Julie Loves Frankie
Sarah Loves Frankie
Debbie Loves Frankie

The cartoon shows the kid turning around as the headlights of a police car pick up the scene. Two cops leap from the prowl car; one reaches for his gun and the other snarls: "O. K., Frankie. The jig's up!"

Miss Sara told me that much about the writer can be learned from the way he scribbles his thoughts on the wall.

"If," she said, "the words or pictures are embellished with curlicues and other ornamental designs, this too becomes significant to the graphologist. If the added-on scribbles are graceful and the faces they use are happy and pretty ones, the graffiti artist is an optimist and has a desire for social companionship.

"But if the scribbles added to the graffiti are messy, with no clear form, and if the faces are done in an ugly manner, the indication is that the writer is not too happy with his own self, and his view of life in general and people in particular may be a very jaundiced one."

Miss Sara, in addition to being a professional graphologist, does freelance writing for publishers of special project books and is accustomed to unusual assignments. One of the most unusual, however, came to her in connection with graffiti.

"I had a phone call from a nun, a principal of a parochial school in mid-Manhattan," Miss Sara told me, "and she wanted me to come over and help her to catch the boys who were writing four-letter words on the walls of the toilet.

"We made a date for the following afternoon. She was waiting for me, a cheerful, chubby nun of middle age. We went up three flights of stairs to the toilet. The nun hung a sign: 'Out of Order, Use the One on the Floor Below' on the knob of the door, and we went into the toilet room.

"The walls were covered with juicy messages based around four-letter words. I felt that the work had been done by four different boys, as I could discern only four styles of printing. From the printing I could deduce how they wrote in cursive script. I told my hostess which boy wrote with squarish formations and which one used a heavy pressure and angular forms. The other two I could see wrote with curvy lines.

"The nun drew from her pocket sixty slips of paper, about three by four inches, and on each was written a sentence: 'This is a sample of my handwriting,' and signed by each boy in the seventh grade, boys of about twelve or thirteen years of age. She said she'd had them write the slips that morning, as part of a penmanship contest.

"She kept peeling off one slip after another, and I was able to pick out four handwritings which I deduced would belong to the four graffiti writers. The nun beamed. She told me that she had suspected the four I had selected, but she'd wanted the expert aid of a handwriting analyst before she took the matter up with the boys.

"She was also very smart in getting 'instant analyses' of most of the handwritings as she flipped over each slip of paper. She'd stop and ask: 'Has this boy good musical sense?' or 'How do you think this boy does in his mathematics?' and so on. Thus, she not only had me help her catch the culprits, but she also got a line on many of the students' abilities."

Miss Sara didn't tell me any of the lines that she found

on the walls of that parochial school, but here are some of the things that our high-school and college students have done in the last year or so:

Work Like Helen Be Happy

Work Fast. Not Half Fast

Lay Down. I Think I Love You

We Are the People Our Parents Warned Us About

I Am a U. C. (Berkeley) Student. Please Do Not Bend, Fold, Spindle or Mutilate Me

Sally Is a Humpty-Dumpty with Hair

Free Pot for All

J. Edgar Hoover Sleeps with a Nite Light

Take LSD and See

Legalize Necrophilia

Apple Pie Makes You Sterile

Eddie Is Crazy Nuts about Dirty Martine, the Dope

To Be Beat Is to Be Cool. To Be Beat-Cool Is NOT to Be Beat. To Be Beat-Cool and Not to Be Beat Is NOWHERE

Support Your Local Police Station—Steal

Fornicate for Freedom

six

IN 79 A.D., MOUNT VESUVIUS ERUPTED AND DESTROYED THE ancient cities of Pompeii and Herculaneum, which were situated in what is now southern Italy. They were in the section known as Campania, a beautiful mountainous region that runs down to the Tyrrhenian Sea and was regarded by rich and distinguished Romans as the finest resort area of its time—sort of a combination of the modern-day Coney Island, Brighton, and Acapulco!

Be that as it may, Pompeii and Herculaneum (particularly Pompeii) were the swinging cities of the time and whenever the Romans were casting about for a good place to vacation, sooner or later somebody would suggest Pompeii or Herculaneum, saying: "Let's go where the action is."

There was only one trouble with these two cities (and nobody gave it a thought at the time). The trouble was that they were located at the foot of Mount Vesuvius, much as Grossinger's, the Concord, and the Nevele today are located in the Catskill Mountains.

And, of course, there came the unpleasant moment when Mount Vesuvius unexpectedly let loose with countless billions of tons of steaming molten lava and completely buried Pompeii and Herculaneum, and the hundreds of villas of the rich, and the forum, the temples, the baths, the theaters, the market places, and thousands of pretty well-heeled Romans, not to mention Pliny the Elder.

At the time, this was looked upon as a hell of a sorry thing, indeed, but, to coin a phrase, it might well have been a blessing in disguise. For the lava rolled over these cities and sealed them in and killed everybody who was there, but—and this is the joyous part—it also sealed in the graffiti on the walls and preserved them for many centuries.

Years later when inquisitive characters broke through the crusty, hardened lava and found the cities beneath, there on the walls were the graffiti just as they'd been written in happier days. Not a single "Joe Loves Dottie" had been destroyed.

And most of the other fine work remained. On the walls of the forum, scientists and classicists found such inscriptions as:

> *Titus Tipples*
>
> *Vespasian Is a Wino*
>
> *Down With Domitian!*
>
> *Up Vesuvius!*

Now, you might not think that this kind of thing would be very valuable, being that it isn't much different from what we have on hand today, but all of the experts in the field have agreed that the graffiti of Pompeii largely has been responsible for giving us insight into the everyday life of that time.

Archeologists, historians, and mythologists, delving into the origins and development of civilization, have made great use of graffiti. And J. Lindsay, who perhaps did most to reconstruct what was cooking in Pompeii before it got thoroughly baked, freely admits that it was the wall writer who told the biggest part of the story.

A learned gentleman I know by the name of John Ferris, writer, historian, world traveler, and a man who has shot more photographs of Philadelphia than any other man in the world, has given attention in recent years to graffiti, and I'd like to give you some of his findings.

"The first makers of graffiti, yielding to man's instinct to express himself," says John, "had no easy time of it. Mostly they worked with a stilo (a stilo is a dagger, and a stiletto is a small dagger), an instrument of bronze or iron, and it was difficult to write with.

"However, in the hands of a man in Pompeii, a stilo was like a pen or a pencil, and it was used to incise on wax tablets such things as letters, accounts, receipts, contracts, and amorous messages. The compulsion to write seems to have been present at all times, and men were less restrained than they are today.

"In a moment of leisure or idleness, a man who came upon a wall or column, then as now, was constrained to set down gossip or bits of intrigue. So we find things like:

Figulus Amat Idaiam

Casesius Fidelis Amat Meconem"

There were, of course, many, many more statements to the effect that Joe loves Dottie—only the Pompeiians didn't know how to spell Joe and Dottie and settled for the amorous linking of such names as Cornelia, Helena, Romulus,

Staphilio, and Modestus. And they didn't confine themselves to romantic writing, says John. There were plenty of malicious and slanderous scribblings about all sorts of people. So, it seems, that in those days if you didn't get a stilo in the back, you got it on your wall.

There were such fascinating jibes as:

Romulus and Remus Are Wolves

Uncle Remus Will Come

Will Romulus Rape the Sabine Women, or Vice Versa?

Romanus Is Queer for Constantine

Flavius Heraclius Isn't in Drag—He Just Looks That Way.

On one of the Roman public baths was lettered:

Occupancy by More Than MCXXXVIII Is Unsanitary—But Very Cozy

49

And on the forum was written:

Draft Nebuchadnezzar

Make Love—Not Punic Wars

Cathartics for Carthage

Tiberius Is a Titmouse

And, on a temple, was scratched:

Adam Clayton Powell Will Yet Come!

John Ferris also points out that graffiti is a name given in Italian art to earthenware which is ornamented by scratching before its second firing. The term, *sgraffiti,* is also used and has the same meaning.

One such graffito that John saw was done by an Etruscan potter named Marcus who wrote in Tyrrheno-Pelasgic characters on an unbaked crater, which is a jar or vase with a wide mouth and a fat belly:

*Iuuna—Laphti—Markei—Kurieas—Kluthi
—Iuke*

That means: "Know you not the skilled potter Mark?"

The implication, of course, is that old Mark was a pretty hot potter and if you didn't know him, brother, well, you just weren't with it. And, what I think is most interesting, is that he apparently thought up that slogan without the aid of Doyle Dane Bernbach, BBD&O, J. Walter Thompson, or any of the other Madison Avenue brains. Probably sold plenty of pots.

John says that one of the most famous graffiti in existence is a caricature of the Crucifixion which was found in 1857 on the wall of the Domus Gelotiana on the Palatine in Rome. It is now in the Kircheriano Museum in the Collegio Romano.

The man on the cross has the head of an ass, and at the side is a praying figure. And there are these words:

Alexamenos Worshiping God

Which gives you a pretty good idea of what somebody thought of poor old Alexamenos.

John reminds us that during Rome's Renaissance period the smarty-type scribblers indulged in a form of graffiti that pleased the citizenry as much as the insult-type stand-up comedians do today. This consisted of a steady exchange of comments, quips, barbs, and salty comments between two statues—Pasquino and Marforio.

Pasquino, now a badly mutilated torso, can be seen today outside the Palazzo Braschi, near the Piazza Navona. Marforio, who has worn better, is in the Campodoglio on the Capitol Hill.

There were other speaking statues in those days—including the figure of the Facchino fountain in the Via Lara and the Babuino in the Via del Babuino—but Pasquino and Marforio were the Amos and Andy of their day.

Pasquino was named for a tailor at whose shop the courtiers, prelates, and the literati gathered daily to gossip, repeat scandal, and tell dirty and/or witty stories. Nobody seems to know whether the tailor himself was a wit who, like Dorothy Parker, was able to stab with both needle and tongue, or whether he merely was happy with having the sayings of others credited to him.

Anyway, a lot of things that were said in his shop were written on something and then taken out and hung on Pasquino—the statue. (Our word, *pasquinade*—anonymous lampoon posted in public—is derived from Pasquino.) The wit more often than not was in the form of a question asked in a two-line verse. And the following day, the answer was found on Marforio on the Capitoline.

Unfortunately, according to John, what seemed mighty funny then, today is as stale as Christopher Columbus' soda biscuits. Or at least we don't have the power of understanding them fully. H. V. Morton, the fine travel writer and authority on Rome, has examined hundreds of these pasquinades only to come to the conclusion that even the poorest Bob Hope and Jerry Lewis gags are 100 per cent funnier.

"Romans," says John, "still yield to the temptation to scrawl a name or a sentiment in public places, although not as freely as do New Yorkers. On my last visit to Rome, I found love messages and drawings of soldiers, guns, and an old-fashioned velocipede on the wall behind the badly worn 'Baboon' in the fountain on Via del Babuino. The Roman subway is spotless, but high in the dome of St. Peter's people for years have been leaving graffiti—mostly names and initials. And one of the names is that of a king of Sweden!"

People of all nations, it seems, cannot resist the urge to scratch up or pencil up public places. So far as I can determine, there is no domain that is pencil pure. Friends of mine who have traveled in the most remote areas of Africa and Asia, and who have toured some sections of the North and South Pole regions, tell me that every once in a while they came upon something, a wall or a tree or simply a signboard stuck in the ice, which proclaims that somebody "was there" or which tells somebody to go home or get the hell out of the area.

There is, for example, a great deal of graffiti in Ireland, a situation which I, for one, find a bit puzzling. Graffiti writers, it is believed, often are driven to write their true feelings on walls because they dare not utter them. But, as we all know, there is nothing that any self-respecting Irishman wouldn't dare to say. So why must he write it too?

Oliver St. John Gogarty dips into the Irish graffiti situation to some extent in his *As I Was Going down Sackville Street*. He tells of a fellow named Thwackhurst, a middle-aged cavalry officer who was an avid collector of Irish graffiti.

Whether there was a real Thwackhurst or not, I don't know. But Dr. Gogarty certainly was real—a physician, writer, and senator—and, much to his dismay, the model for the plump Buck Mulligan of James Joyce's *Ulysses*.

Dr. Gogarty tells of meeting Thwackhurst near the Mansion House in Dawson Street, Dublin, and asking how his graffiti collection was coming along.

Thwackhurst complains bitterly that political scribblings are all but obliterating the really good, witty, and exciting graffiti that he seeks. He moans that it's almost impossible to find anything but dreary scribblings about politics.

And this, he contends, indicates that Ireland is in a bad way.

"It's always a sign of decline in the fortunes of a country," he says. "Even at their moments of ease, the people are obsessed with thoughts of politics."

Dr. Gogarty asks Thwackhurst to give him a good example of the kind of graffiti he prefers, an example of Dublin's Golden Age of Graffiti. He starts to fumble for his notebook, but even before he pulls it out he recites:

> *"Here lies the grave of Keelin,*
> *And on it his wife is kneeling;*
> *If he were alive, she would be lying*
> *And he would be kneeling."*

This little example doesn't exactly set the good doctor on fire, but Thwackhurst doggedly defends it. "It is fundamental," he says. "It expresses the differences between Life and Death, Love and Loss. It is touched with the *lacrimae rerum* above the Weeping Wall. Terse as a Greek epitaph."

Gogarty then reminds him that there is a graffito about

Shank's patent in Trinity College and Thwackhurst says he'll dash off there and copy it. Gogarty mentions the baths of Caracalla and says that the walls must have been covered with wonderful graffiti written by the young men as they lay there cooling during the Silver Age of Rome.

What would be Latin for?:

Dial Soap Makes You Smell Good

Duz Does Everything

Don't Make Waves

Bring On the Naked Dames!

Anyway, Gogarty asks Thwackhurst where he found the Keelin epitaph, and he says:

"In the lavatory behind Nelson's pillar."

Then, expressing the true graffiti collector's disgust at pallid imitations of classic inscriptions, he shakes his head and says:

"There is a version in a pub in Dalkey—but it's corrupt!"

seven

WHAT IS BELIEVED TO BE THE OLDEST GRAFFITI IN THE NEW World was discovered only a few months ago on the rock walls of a Mexican cave in the State of Guerrero, about seventy-five miles northeast of Acapulco in the Sierra Madre del Sur.

Two amateur American anthropologists made the find—three paintings and three line drawings which are believed to have been executed somewhere between 400 B.C. and 800 B.C. by artists among the Olmec people. The Olmecs generally are credited with being the first high culture in the Western Hemisphere. They antedated or were contemporary with the Mayas.

These paintings and sketches—vividly depicting human beings and serpents—are, of course, practically modern when compared with the ancient cave paintings of bison and reindeer discovered many years ago in Spain and France. They, reportedly, were painted somewhere around 15,000 B.C.

The Olmec paintings were found by Carlo T. E. Gay, a retired executive of New York City, and Gillett G. Griffin, curator of graphic arts at the Princeton University Library.

They and other experts in the field contend that the paintings—in red, yellow, green, black, and white—are about three hundred years older than the oldest previously discovered paintings in the Americas. These are wall paint-

55

ings in Tikal, Guatemala, which have been dated at between 100 B.C. and the birth of Christ.

Messrs. Gay and Griffin said that the Olmec paintings are located between 3,400 and 4,000 feet inside the Mexican cave, which is called Juxtlahuaca. One painting shows two figures engaged in what is believed to be a kind of Olmec ritual.

One of the figures, the larger, is five feet five inches tall, has shoulder-length black hair, and a beard. He holds a trident-shaped implement in his right hand and a serpent, or serpent-like staff in his left.

DE LOS ULTIMOS
ROJOS CALIENTES
INDIOS*

* LAST OF THE RED
HOT MAYAS

All of which shows that we haven't gained much over the ages. This figure obviously is an early hippie, with the long hair and beard. The only way we've advanced, it seems to me, is that the latter-day hippie ignored the trident and serpent, and held a banana and a copy of a psychedelic magazine.

There is a barely visible motif, shaped like an 8, in front of the trident, which indicates there was more to the design and that there were probably some words, or what passed for words in those days, explaining what the painting was about, or, more likely, making some uncomplimentary remarks about the figure himself. Such as:

Last of the Red Hot Mayas

Unfair to Barbers (signed) *Local #6*

Louie Sleeps with Snakes

Up Trident!

Unfortunately, however, we probably never will know for sure just what sentiment was expressed by the Olmec grafficionados. We do know, however, a great deal about what was scribbled on the walls in London in the early eighteenth century and for this we are indebted to a gentlenamed Hurlo Thrumbo, an editor and collector of graffiti.

In 1731 he published a set of four small books called: *The Merry Thought: or, the Glaſs Window and Bog-Houſe Miſcellany.* Thrumbo got his graffiti from scribbles in the bog houses, or toilets, and, most interestingly, from scratches on drinking glasses and windows in taverns— scratches that had been made by diamonds!

He describes his book on the title page as:

"Taken from The Original Manuſcripts written in Diamond by Perſons of the firſt Rank and Figure in Great Britain; relating to Love, Matrimony, Drunkenneſs, Sobriety, Ranting, Scandal, Politicks, Gaming, and many other Subjects, Serious and Comical.

"Faithfully tranſcribed from the Drinking-Glaſſes and Windows in the ſeveral noted Taverns, Inns and other Publick Places in this Nation. Amongſt which are intermixed the Lucubrations of the polite Part of the World, written upon Walls in Bog-houſes, etc."

He then went on to state that it would be "a great pity"

if the profound learning and wit of ſo many illuſtrious
perſonages, who had favoured the publick with their lucubrations, "ſhould be loſt to the world!"

He handed himself a mighty bouquet right at the start
by saying:

"How many Accidents might rob us of theſe ſparkling
pieces, if the induſtrious Care of the Collector had not
taken this Way of preſerving them, and handing them to
Poſterity? In the firſt Place, ſome careleſs Drawer breaks
the Drinking-Glaſſes inſcribed to the Beauties of our Age;
a furious Mob at Election breaks the windows of a contrary
Party; and a cleanly Landlord muſt have, forſooth, his
Rooms new-painted and white-waſh'd every now and then,
without regarding in the leaſt the Wit and Learning he is
obliterating." (Shades of Santini!)

Then, dedicating his book to "The Honourable and
Worthy Authors of the Following Curious Pieces," Thrumbo

58

uses a fistful of words to state that he isn't *stealing* these worthy but curious pieces of writing as many others publishers have done "without acknowledging the Piracy they are guilty of." Oh, no, not Thrumbo. He clearly states that he is "not the Daw in the Fable, that would vaunt and ſtrut in your Plumes."

"And beſides," he says, "I know very well you might have me upon the Hank, according to Law, and treat me as a Highwayman or Robber; for you might ſafely ſwear upon your Honours, that I had ſtole the whole book from your recreative Minutes. But I am more generous; I am what you may call Frank and Free; I acknowledge them to be YOURS, and now publiſh them to perpetuate the Memory of your Honours Wit and Learning; But as everyone muſt have ſomething of Self in him, I am violently flattered that my Character will ſhine like the Diamonds you wrote with, under your exalted Protection, to the End of Time."

He signed it: "Your Moſt Humble, Moſt Obedient, Moſt Obſequious, Moſt Devoted, and Moſt Faithful Servant. Hurlo Thrumbo."

And, having set forth all these little pleasantries, he got right down to publishing some of the dirtiest lines and rhymes to be found in all of England!

I will say this: none of it is of the low American school that specializes in short, simple sentences and batches of four-letter words. Ah, no. All of it, even though dealing with fornication, adultery, perversion, and various bizarre subjects that defy classification, is well thought out, witty, impudent, titillating, and generally in verse. In fact, some of the verses are composed of many stanzas—providing that people had lots more time in those days, and that the diamonds were harder than the ones they're whipping up today. A *modern* diamond would wear out after only three or four of those sizzling poems.

Let's take a look at some of the "cleaner" bog-house literature—

From the White-Hart Inn at Acton:

> Kitty's the ſtrangeſt Girl in Life,
> For any one to make a Wife;
> Her Conſtitution's cold, with warm Deſire
> She kiſſes juſt like Ice and Fire.

On a tavern window in Fleet Street:

> No more let each fond foppling court a
>   Brother,
> And quit the Girls to dreſs for one another;
> Old maids, in Vengeance to their ſlighted
>   Beauty,
> Shall one Day make you wiſh you'd done your
>   Duty;
> Thro' Hell they drag ye on moſt aukward
>   Shapes,
> Yoak'd in their Apron-Strings, and led for
>   Apes.

60

On a window in Mainwaring's Coffee House in Fleet Street:

> *If Kiffes were the only Joys in Bed,*
> *Then Women would with one another wed.*

On a window at the Catherine-Wheel in High-Wickham—

> *Salley's my Toaft from Head to Tail;*
> *Not half fo good is Toaft and Ale.*

On a window at the Red Lion in Southwell—

> *Clarinda lay here, with a young Cavalier:*
> *With her heart full of Fear, for her Hufband*
> *was near.*

And under that was written:

> *'Tis very true; for we faw Rem-in-Re*
> *through the Key-Hole*
> *(signed) S. M., J. M., R. H., Feb 3, 1728.*

In Ben Jonson's time there was a tavern called "The Sign of the Angel," run by a Mrs. Hope and her daughter Prudence. Jonson went there a lot and some years later when he visited it again, he found different people in charge. Then he wrote:

> *When Hope and Prudence kept this Houfe,*
> *The Angel kept the door;*
> *Now Hope is dead,*
> *And the Angel fled,*
> *And Prudence turn'd a Whore*

At the Swan in Chelsea:

> *Jenny demure with prudifh Looks,*
> *Turns up her Eyes, and rails at naughty*
> *Folks;*

61

But in a private Room, turns up her lech'rous Tail,
And kiffes till fhe's in for Cakes and Ale.

At the Toy in Hampton Court:

Damn Molley H——ns for her Pride
She'll fuffer none but Lords to ride;
But why the Devil fhould I care,
Since I can find another Mare?

At the Star in Coventry:

I'll never get drunk again,
For my Head's full of Pain,
And it grieves me to think,
That by Dint of good Drink,
I fhould lie with my Phillis in vain.
(signed) R. H. 1712

At the Tuns in Cambridge:

At Home Mifs Molly's fcarce fifteen,
Mama fays fhe's no more;
But if the Parifh-Book fays true,
Mifs Molly's thirty-four.

From the Red Lyon at Egham:

She that thinks upon her Honour
Needs no other Guard upon her.

Written underneath was:

She that has a Man upon her,
Never thinks upon her honour.

On Harrison's window at Bath:

I Kifs'd her ftanding, Kifs'd her lying,
Kifs'd her in Health, and Kifs'd her dying;

62

*And when fhe mounts the Skies, I'll kifs her
flying.*

Under that was written:

Well faid, my Boy.

In the Trinity College vaults is a tobacco box with this
inscription:

Pandora's Treafure

Under this is written:

> *Tobacco, that outlandifh Weed,*
> *It dries the Brain, and fpoils the Seed;*
> *It dulls the Spirit, it dims the Sight,*
> *It robs a Woman of her Right.*

In a window of a public house near Tunbridge:

> *Sing High Ding a Ding,*
> *And Ho Ding a Ding,*
> *I'm finely brought to Bed;*
> *My Lord has ftole that troublefome Thing,*
> *That Folks call a Maidenhead.*
> *(signed) Jane Hughs, eighteen years of age.*

In a window at Lebeck's-Head:

> *He that loves a Glafs without a G,*
> *Leave out L, and that is he*

There's a very long poem that was printed on the wall
of a bog-house and it's described in Thrumbo's book as
being about "A Friar who cuckol'd a Dyer at Roan in
France; and the Dyer's revenge in dying him Blue."

That poem's a bit racy for this gentle volume, but I do
think we can turn off Mr. Thrumbo with the following

exchange inscribed on a window of the Peacock at North-ampton:

> *I love dear Betty and Betty loves me;*
> *And it ſhall not be long before marry'd*
> *   we be.*

Under this was written:

> *If you muſt make a Rhime upon your Laſs,*
> *I'll make another—Rhimer kiſs my A—ſe.*

eight

I AM DEEPLY INDEBTED FOR ALL THE PRECEDING BOG-HOUSE material to my friend, Allen Walker Read, professor of English at Columbia University, linguistic expert, and outstanding authority on American folklore. It was he who first told me about *The Merry-Thought* booklets and, indeed, provided me with photostats of the only known complete copies, which are at Oxford.

And I am indebted to Professor Read for much more than that, as you'll presently see. First, however, let me tell you that I believe the professor was one of the first Americans, if not *the* first, to probe the field of graffiti in a big way.

Back in 1928, he took an extensive sight-seeing trip throughout the western United States and Canada and, of course, saw lots of graffiti in men's rooms, on restaurant walls, and in many other places.

"It was borne in upon me," he says, "that these inscriptions are a form of folklore that should be made the subject of a scholarly study." And so he copied down just about all the graffiti that came to his attention. Then, in 1935, he had privately printed in Paris a limited number of copies of a pamphlet entitled: "Lexical Evidence from Folk Epigraphy in Western North America, a Glossarial Study of the Low Element in the English Vocabulary."

This study, a most serious one, mind you, is filled with all the four-letter words known to English-speaking people, countless feelthy inscriptions, and even more dirty rhymes than you can find in *The Merry-Thought*.

This might seem like a less-than-dignified pursuit for a staid and gentlemanly professor of one of the world's most distinguished universities, but, as any professor and researcher will tell you, it ain't no good to just go halfway. It's the truth, the whole truth, and nothing but the truth, so help you God—or the whole project isn't worth anything.

"It is characteristic of the folklorist," says Professor Read, "that he can take unpromising, trivial details, organize them into an orderly body of material, and from them derive significant findings in the interpretation of human life."

And in a paper delivered before the American Folklore Society's annual meeting in Denver in 1965, the professor maintained that, although some people contend that epigraphy is folklore only by courtesy, "the random writings on the walls are a valid form of folklore."

"They are the product of the folk," he said. "Though they very seldom have literary value, they afford insight into folk attitudes."

He said that "the writing of graffiti has a long and honorable history" and that it "was likely to occur very frequently in ancient times because personal writing materials were not easy of access and walls could serve."

"So ephemeral is this material," he said, "that very few examples survive from recent centuries. One incident can be noted from England in 1596. In that year, Sir John Harrington, in his 'Metamorphosis of Ajax,' recounted the plight of 'a faire Lady' who had dirtied her clothes by a bowel movement, and he continued: 'a serving man . . . that could not keepe counsell had spyed it, & wrote in the grossest terms it could be exprest, upon a wall, what he had seen.' "

The American Indian, apparently, didn't give a damn about graffiti (he had plenty of other things to do) but, according to the professor, graffiti in America began quite early as a result of Spanish explorers leaving their names and dates on El Morro, the jutting shoulder of rock in New Mexico. It is now a national monument, with the oldest inscriptions covered by glass.

Professor Read said that in this connection, Daniel Boone's carving on a beech tree in 1760 along a stage road in central Tennessee is memorable. It was legible for more than a century, and it read:

D. Boon
Cilled A BAR
in ThE
yEAR 1760

But not all early American inscriptions were so simple and so innocuous. Plenty of lusty language appeared everywhere and quite a few of the more respectable citizens complained—for all the good that did.

In 1839, according to Professor Read, a Boston Brahmin, G. F. Thayer, issued a blast against the epigraphy that he believed to be blanketing Boston. He said in a lecture:

"We cannot escape the evidence of this, which assails us on every hand, sometimes on the very walls of our schoolhouses and churches; but especially in places removed from *public* view, where the most shocking obscenity of language is displayed, to poison the youthful mind, illustrated by emblems, which, in the words of one who deeply mourns with us over the existence of this monstrous evil, this desolating curse, *'would make a heathen blush!'*

"These frightful assaults on decency demand reform.

The deep, low murmur of insulted humanity will, I doubt not, unless this evil be checked, ascend to the tribunal of Eternal Purity, and invoke the malediction of our Judge, which may yet be displayed in the blasting of our fair land, like another Sodom!

"To avert so deplorable a catastrophe, let the thousands of the good and virtuous in your midst, formed into one indomitable phalanx, take the noble stand which belongs to them, and never abandon it, till the enemy be forever vanquished, forever banished from the now polluted, but ever to be cherished land of the Pilgrims."

Well, that's part of what the good Brahmin said, and I can see that he really got stirred up. But I particularly like what Professor Read said in his lecture after reciting the whole thing:

"An impassioned attack of this sort was his only way of recording his fascination with the subject. How much more would we honor him if he had only copied down the inscriptions for the edification of posterity!"

Fortunately, I have a few of those shocking inscriptions and for your benefit and Professor Read's I'll reproduce some of the cleaner ones here:

Queen Victoria Isn't Up to Snuff

Martin Van Buren Is Still Nuts About Dolley Madison

Bobby Kennedy Wears a Whig

George Washington Lives and Makes Coffee

Free the Erie Canal

Up Your Alimentary Canal!

Professor Read really got bitten by the graffiti bug and hasn't lost interest in the subject in forty years. And, in common with virtually all students of graffiti, he never has seen anybody in the act of giving birth to a graffito. He isn't sure just who's responsible for the writing.

"From internal evidence, however," he said, "one can say that the range of the epigraphers is wide—from the uneducated and illiterate to the sophisticated and intellectual. And the importance of what they write is in revealing folk attitudes in a variety of areas. Especially they record dissentient opinion that is not acceptable to 'the establishment' or 'respectable' members of society."

After Professor Read returned from his 1928 exploration of the western United States and Canada, he compiled his findings and made up the booklet that was privately printed. He noted on the title page that circulation was to be restricted to "students of linguistic, folklore, abnormal psychology, and allied branches of the social sciences." And he warned that the scribbles reproduced therein were not for weak stomachs.

"Judged merely as reading matter," he wrote, "the following work is abominably, incredibly obscene, and the compiler begs that any one will lay this book down who is not prepared to look at all social phenomena with the dispassionate eye of the anthropologist and the student of abnormal psychology. I believe that no emanation of the human spirit is too vile or too despicable to come under the record and analysis of the scientist.

"The late Professor William Graham Sumner, in the introduction to his famous *Folkways* (Boston, 1907) recognized into what devious channels a study of folk material might lead, and folk epigraphy should be approached with his warning in mind: 'I must add that if any one is liable to be shocked by *any* folkways he ought not to read about folkways at all. "Nature her custom holds, let shame say what it will." (*Hamlet*, IV, 7).' "

Professor Read, in his tour, concentrated mostly on the writing found in toilets, on the presumption that inasmuch as the material there has no inhibition as to vulgarity and obscenity, "it throws light upon one aspect of the American people."

"On these walls," said the professor, "are recorded sentiments and words that are usually kept alive only by word of mouth. The inscriptions are fugitive, for spring coats of paint obliterate them wholesale, yet they remain the documentary source for otherwise oral material."

The professor found that the graffiti writers had countless motivations. One of the main reasons, he said, is the well-known human yearning to leave a record of one's presence or one's existence. Like these graffiti he found in western tourist camps and railroad stations:

> *A. W. Smith Grahm Ky*
> *broke and trying to get home*
> *dont it beat hell*
>
> *Were from Chicago and Damn Proud of It*
>
> *The Yodeling Cowboy*
> *from Texas*

There are also people who have such strong feelings
against seeing writing in public places that they themselves
write on walls. Like:

Fools' names are like their faces
Always seen in public places

Anybody Who Writes on Walls Is Nuts

Don't Scribble on This Wall

Please Help Me Stop Writing on Walls

In some instances, the professor said, the epigrapher is
simply imbued with an idea that must find expression. At
Madison River Camp, Yellowstone National Park, he found
this lament from a man who'd been reading a guide pamphlet:

*There Is No Fishing Here. The Book is a
Dam Liar*

Many graffitists, of course, are protesting something and have no other way of making their feelings noticeable:

*LBJ Thinks He Is Intelligant but He's Just
Stoopid*

New York Made ME *Dirty Today*

New York Is a Summer Vegetable

Help Police Brutality

None of the above, of course, were found by Professor Read. All are contemporary, written on subway walls, toilets, and advertising posters. But the professor found some much like them, nearly forty years ago:

Al Smith Is a Son of a Bitch

*May Itching Piles Torment You and Corns
Grow on Your Feet*

*The Miners came in 49, the whores in 51
They jumbled a mess together and called it
the Native Son*

*The Capitalists Built and Gave This Library
to the Public*

I'll Kill the Son of a Bitch Who Wrote This

But the great bulk of what the professor found had to do with sex and other bodily functions. Things like these admonitions over urinals:

Bulls with Short Horns Stand Up Close

Little drops of water upon the toilet floor
Uses lots of elbow grease and makes the
porter sore
So now kind friends remember, before the
water flows,
Please adjust the distance according to your
hose.

And many, many things involving sex, heterosexual, homosexual, perverted, inverted, converted and, I think, even upverted—whatever that is.

But if you think I'm going to print any of *that* stuff—even in the interest of pure science—you all is very, very wrong.

However, I will tell you about what Professor Read found in London and New York when he continued his investigations a few years ago.

nine

ON A RECENT TRIP TO LONDON, PROFESSOR READ FOUND THAT the graffiti there are similar in many ways to those found in New York and other American cities, although there are some differences.

One of the similarities is that the rivalry of boys' gangs is expressed just as heartily as in New York.

In New York you'll find such things as:

The Falcons Is Supreem

Avengers Forever

The Purple Dragons Are Chicken

Kill the Brownsville Brownies

Girl Gangs Stink

In London, the professor found:

Mods Are Fab

Stamp Out Rockers

The Mods Will Hit Again

The last line, by the way, was altered by somebody who put an S in front of "Hit."

75

THE MODS WILL HIT AGAIN

He found most of the political inscriptions were anti-Labour:

> *Labour Get Out*
>
> *Wogs for Neighbour—Vote Labour*
>
> *If You Want a Brothal Next Door, Vote Labour*

There are many racial inscriptions telling the Negroes and the Jews what they should do and where they should go, and the Irish are still collecting their share of vituperation. Oddly enough, the professor says that there's little anti-American sentiment, although in connection with the general unhappiness over Viet Nam he saw:

> *!!Abandon Ship*
> *Yanks!!*
> *Viet Nam*

The graffiti dealing with sex, he says, are much less frequent and less raw than those in New York. "The principal manifestations," he said, "are isolated 'bad words' and pictographs of genitalia, and the pictures of romantic couples on advertising posters sometimes are adorned with balloons containing (rare) speech."

There's a widespread advertisement for lipstick that bears the question: "What exactly makes a Frenchwoman so French?" and many answers have been written under that, including:

Le Bon Oomph

B. O.

That She Is Not English, Fortunately

In England, as elsewhere, the professor points out, "the great bulk of graffiti has very little sociological significance beyond the assertion of individuality—the record that a certain person was at a certain place. In the continuum of history, someone thereby has captured his own instant of time. Typical of the personal graffiti he saw are:

Yinka Loves Josie

Gunilla Is a Very Sweet Little Girl

Eccles Loves Chips in Brown Gravy

But, he says, as an American he was baffled by this one, found in Piccadilly Circus station:

I Am a
Little Gnome!!
I am a Super
Little
Gnomette!

In the early 1960s, Professor Read spent a good deal of time snooping about New York, inspecting advertising posters in the city subways, and he reaped a rich and raunchy collection.

"My collections, however," he said, "are somewhat distorted in the direction of the intellectual, for my richest sources have been in the subway stations near Columbia University, and many of them evidently were done by students waiting for their trains.

"Each gleaning at an interval of about three months has yielded a fresh new crop. In one instance I even found a graffito in Latin. Near the inscription "Big Brother Is Watching You" someone else had provided the translation:

Magnus Frater Te Spectat

Much of what the professor collected is in the "I was here" category. "At first blush," he said, "this seems to have little sociological significance, but perhaps we should take second thoughts about that. The urge to assert one's individuality by capturing a particular moment in time and space is so pervasive as to account for the most prevalent kind of graffiti, wherever people congregate."

He says that a very frequent formula in New York which did not occur several decades ago in the West is as follows:

Rose was here
but now is gone
but left her name
to carry on

Others of that type are:

Harry (The Hustler) Was Here

Mr. Sure Was Here

Julio Was Here. Don't Bother Him

Sometimes, the professor says, special personalities will shine through, and thus we have:

Robert Sayer
&
Anne Cully
were here & gave this subway station the
dignity it should always have

Another graffito of this kind offers a peculiar psychology:

I Was Not Here

In the declaration-of-love field, the professor found:

Lucky loved Blanche
but she's gone
Now there's Terry
that gives Lucky the love
how it turns out
only God knows

I Love Nance—I think

Billy the Lover
There Is No Other

Who Loves Sara Piavia
Deserves Her

I Love My Mother

Under which was written in another hand:

> *O.K., Mommy*

In the folk humor field, which the professor says consists more often of low-grade word-play that is relished by the unsophisticated, we find:

> *Will mothers love their*
> *2 headed children twice*
> *as much?*

> *Q: What do you give an elephant that has*
> *Dirhyea?*
> *A: You give it* ROOM

> *May We Join you?*

Under, in another hand:

> *I Didn't Know I Was Falling Apart*

A prescription was on one poster:

> *For a cold—*
> *Put your hat on the table*
> *& drink whiskey until you see 3 hats*

And the professor found this well-known verse:

> *My favorite teacher took a drink*
> *But he will drink no more*
> *For what he thought was H_2O*
> *Was H_2SO_4*

The theatrical advertisement for *What Makes Sammy Run?* brought many answers, the professor says, such as these:

> *Ex-Lax*

Castro Oil

His Wife

And when Sammy Davis Jr. was starring in *Golden Boy,* somebody wrote on the advertising poster:

> *There Seems to Be an Ethiopian in the Fuel Supply*

One day the professor saw the following lettered on a poster in the subway:

> *A Watched Proverb Butters No Parsnips!*

Then at intervals of three or four days, these lines were added in different handwritings:

> *A Buttered Parsnip Watches No Proverbs Either*
>
> *A Buttered Watch Parsnips No Proverbs*
>
> *Melted Butter Never Watches Parsnips*
>
> *A Parsniped Butter Proverbs No Grunch but the Eggplant Over There*
>
> *A Panned Pars Nips No Butter*

Once he found, in reversed or mirror writing, this frantic plea:

> **Help! I Am Trapped Behind This Sign!**

In the field of graffiti dealing with religion, Professor Read was surprised at the antagonism aroused by a series of printed advertising posters for religion. One of the posters which read: "Worship Together This Week" set off these reactions:

Is It Your Business?

Dont
Advertise
Religion

Keep Our God
Free of
Churches

A poster which had an arrow pointing to a church steeple got decorated in this manner:

Dear Madison Ave:
  Please reserve
Phallic advertising
Methods for cigarettes
and beer.
    Thank you

Satirizing the familiar line: "The Family That Prays Together Stays Together," some smarty wrote:

The Family That Shoots Together,
Loots Together

Under "What is the difference between God and Santa Claus?" somebody scribbled:

There Is a Santa Claus

Another bitter comment:

MAN *Created God in His Image*

And, to a poster which proclaimed "Call on Jesus Now," a helpful soul appended:

82

If No One Answers, Leave a Message at the
Candy Store

There were many comments about who God is and where
he is:

God Is 300% American

I Found God in Gimbel's

God Is an Atheist

God Twinkles and Shines

God Is NOT *Dead. He's Just Very Sick and*
Evil Works

God Is Alive in Argentina

God Is Dead—Nietzche

Nietzche Is Dead—God

Who Cares?—Moses

Me—God

In the area of philosophic ideals, the professor found:

Today is the tomorrow
You worried about yesterday

I care Not for the Song & Dance,
The City Lights & the Laughter,
Give me the Quiet Countryside &
Simple Human Hearts

Did you know that for
every pound of idiocy in
your head your soul
has to travel three
more light-years?

All Artists Remain Children

Man Needs Anarchy

Hyperventilation Cures Hypertension

We're slapped on the ass
to give us the breath
To start us off on our march
toward death

So whatever happens, Happens!
So whoever dies just dies
So what the Hell!

In the lush field of sex, the professor did quite well, although not so well as one might do in the toilets. There's less preoccupation with sex on subway posters, but some of the examples still are pretty good:

One day the professor saw this written on a wall:

I Am a Virgin

The next time he saw it, somebody had inserted the word "Former" between "a" and "Virgin."

Another inscription he caught appeared under this line in an advertisement for a thrift shop:
"Where do good minks go after they leave Park Avenue?"

To the Whore House

Other samples:

Sal Is a Sex Maniac

I'm a Queer

Marvin Is a Fagot

Womens Are for the Birds

And, in the field of pleas for support of worthy causes, he found:

Join the Fight Against Ingrown Toenails

Help Stamp Out Entropy

Help Stamp Out Whooping Cranes

Support Supports
Buy a Jock

Help Wipe Out Humans—Support Your
Local Tax Collector

ten

PROFESSOR READ, OF COURSE, ISN'T THE ONLY LEARNED gentleman who has made a study of graffiti. Some of the people who have written about it, in addition to Kinsey, Reisner, and Freeman whom I've already quoted, include:

John Pudney, author of *The Smallest Room*; John G. Bourke, *Scatalogic Rites of All Nations*; Gershon Legman, *The Horn Book: Studies in Erotic Folklore and Bibliography*; Henrich Fischer and Dr. von Waldheim, authors of several papers on *"Skatologische Inschriften"*; Reginald Reynolds, *Cleanliness and Godliness*; Lawrence Wright, *Clean and Decent;* J. Lindsay, *The Writing on the Wall,* and Helen H. Tanzer, *The Common People of Pompeii— A Study of Graffiti.*

Most recently several other distinguished educators have dipped into the field and I want to tell you about them and what they discovered.

Alan Dundes, Ph.D., is one whose research is contained in a splendid paper: "Here I Sit—A Study of American Latrinalia." An associate professor of anthropology and folklore at the University of California at Berkeley, he describes himself as a "folklorist by training and a Freudian by choice." Among his more conventional publications is an anthology, *The Study of Folklore*, published by Prentice-Hall in 1965.

Professor Dundes declares:

"Despite the widespread distribution of [graffiti] and despite the fact that many of them are demonstrably traditional, one looks in vain for *extended* collections of published texts and for any rational discussion of them or the practice of writing them.

"Most histories of the water closet (e.g., Pudney, Reynolds, Wright) do little more than recognize that such traditions exist. Typical is the remark made by the poet, John Pudney, who in writing *The Smallest Room*, bothers to say: 'I must here resist the temptation urged on me by several men of letters to quote more freely from this poetry of the smallest room.' "

Professor Dundes, incidentally, believes that the word "graffiti" is too broad for his specialty—the inscriptions found in toilets—inasmuch as graffiti include all kinds of writing and marks placed on walls, fences, buildings, etc. So, he proposes that the term "latrinalia" might be better to describe his water closet poetry, words, and sketches.

The professor declares regretfully that American social scientists simply have failed to give anything like adequate study to this kind of material.

He finds it curious that nobody thinks you're nuts if you study the graffiti—or the latrinalia—of the past, but people give you the funny eye if you start putting modern-day toilet-wall scribbles under the magnifying glass.

An archaeologist, he points out, is expected to go grubbing around in the bowels of the earth, poring over the remains of men and what they produced. Physical anthropologists are free to, and, indeed, are expected to, poke into every part of the human body and lay portions of it out for contemplative study. Ethnographers can go into what they euphemistically call "the field"—tribal whorehouses, pagan palaces, etc.—and voyeuristically observe what I shall delicately describe as "exotic customs."

But, if these scientists watched similar antics in their own culture, they'd be nothing but dirty old men and probably would get bagged by the local cops.

So it is that a similar taint, according to the professor, hangs over the heads of those scientists who are interested in how we Americans go potty. He wonders how, when, and where these acts are performed. He has searched many an ethnography and found no reference to these daily necessities. He implies that just because you and I know what *we* do, there's no reason to believe that *everybody* does the same thing the same way—and, he stoutly insists, the ethnographer, in making his study of man, absolutely must include *all* aspects of human activity.

And what better or more joyous place to find indications of what we do in lavatories than in the johns themselves? He maintains that the study of latrinalia is "clearly a legitimate area of inquiry because one must not forget that it is humans who write on bathroom walls and humans who read these writings."

He quotes Reynolds: "Stereotyped and crude, our lavatory inscriptions are the measure of our social fixations; that enterprising anthropologist who is said to be collecting photographs of them in all parts of the world should reveal more of the truth than all of the bombastic historians who will so soon be clothing our grotesque society with dignified phrases and political stercorations, representing its present antics as studied movements, to be explained in terms of high principles and rational conduct."

I'm not sure I'm well enough educated to understand just what the learned gentleman had in mind with all those erudite phrases, but I think he means that one picture of a graffito that reads: "Pee Pee on De Gaulle" reveals more about America's feeling for Le Grand Charles than 10,000 words.

Professor Dundes suggests that more graffiti are found in toilets than anywhere else because toilets give you more privacy and freedom from the normal restraints of the adult world than any other place. And, he says, the very fact that there has to be some sexual exposure in the toilet gets the mind off the problems at the office and focuses it on some of the things that various human flutterbies would like to do—if they dared.

The professor's studies have led him to break down toilet writings into five main categories. We have one big department that includes advertisements or solicitations, generally of a sexual nature. Then there's the area of requests or commands, more often than not concerning the mechanics of what you're in the toilet to do. Lots of graffiti are devoted to directions, usually false or facetious. Many more are commentaries, contributed either by the establishment or the clients, and the fifth category is composed of personal laments and introspective musings.

The good professor gives some examples of the "want-ad" class that, unfortunately, I don't think my publisher will let me pass on to you. However, here are some I've seen myself:

> *Call MU 2-0000 If You Want a New Sweetie.*
> *I'll Come in Drag*
>
> *If You've Got What I Want, Meet Me at Broadway and 43rd St., 9* P.M., *Any Thursday. Wear a Gardenia*
>
> *You Never Really Had It Until I Give It to You.*
> *Call Tommie, PL 5-0000*
>
> *I Want Something* BIG. *Write Your Phone Number Here*
>
> *Anybody Want My Sister? Call TR 7-0000*

Professor Dundes lists these standard admonitions:

> *Don't throw cigarette butts in the urinal—*
> *It makes them soggy and hard to light*
>
> *Please do not throw butts in the urinal—*
> *Do we piss in your ash trays?*
> *The Management*
>
> *Here is the place we all must come*
> *To do the work that must be done.*
> *Do it quick and do it neat—*
> *But please don't do it on the seat*

Smile, You're on Candid Camera

In the directions category, the professor lists:

In Case of Atomic Attack, Hide under this Urinal.
It Hasn't Been Hit Yet!

Directions to get to Texas:
Go west until you smell crap—that's Oklahoma.
Then go south until you step in it—that's Texas

(Scribbled on the ceiling):

While You're Reading this,
You're Peeing on Your Shoes

In the commentaries area, the professor offers:

You Are Holding the Future of America in Your Hands

No matter how you dance and prance,
The last two drops go down your pants

No need to stand on the toilet seat
The crabs in this place jump 40 feet

The heat of the meat is inversely proportional to the angle of the dangle

Most of the poetry falls into the laments or introspective musings department:

Here I sit, broken-hearted—
Paid a nickel, only f——

Here I sit in stinking vapor
Some sunuvabitch stole the toilet paper

Sam, Sam, the janitor man
Chief superintendent of the crapping can

91

He washes out the bowls and picks up the towels
And listens to the roar of other men's bowels

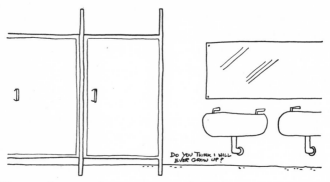

The professor, of course, speculates to some extent in his paper as to why people write latrinalia. He points out that Reynolds stated that generations of lavatory wall writers simply write for the pleasure of breaking a taboo, presumably the taboo of referring to body elimination activities.

And he quotes Professor Read as suggesting that latrinalia probably results from many different motivations, including "the well-known yearning to leave a record of one's presence or one's existence."

In addition, however, Professor Dundes explains that psychoanalyst Ernest Jones thinks it's basically something else. He thinks it's a primitive smearing impulse.

Infants, as we all know, love to take anything that comes to hand and smear it on the wall. Their decorating material includes such things as spinach, strained carrots, pudding, mush, and if their diapers aren't attended to quickly enough, much worse.

Now parents who prevent this pleasant pastime might well be squelching a desire for fulfillment, artistic or otherwise, which later will blossom into full-blown graffiti.

Jones has stated that people who carve or write their names are leaving not only a memento of themselves, but something that might injure or spoil a beautiful object. (If you can't smear spinach, scratch mahogany!) And he suggests that dirty words upon the wall are really dirt themselves, independent of the dirtiness of their meaning.

"Using words, dirty words," he says, "some individuals finally do give vent to the impulse to sully walls. Since 'dirt' is supposed to be deposited in the clean, white receptacles found in bathrooms, what more flagrant act of rebellion than to place symbolic dirt on the very walls surrounding the receptacles!"

In all of the research papers I've read on the collecting of graffiti, I've found nothing that refers to what an arduous task it is (although Reisner did say he washed his hands fifty times a day) except in a paper "The Handwriting on the Wall" prepared by Lee Sechrest of Northwestern University and Luis Flores of the University of the Philippines. These poor fellows had a hell of a time!

Their investigations, first of all, had to do largely with homosexuality among graffiti writers, and the difference between the character and quantity of that kind of graffiti in America and the Philippines. While that is all very interesting, it's not something we need to go into here. It's sufficient, I think, to say that the Sechrest-Flores team found that in the American sampling, 42 per cent of all inscriptions involved homosexuality in some way, while only 2 per cent of Filipino inscriptions concerned homosexuality at all.

What fascinated me about the Sechrest-Flores report was the difficulties the researchers encountered. To begin with, they had problems in selecting the toilets.

There before them lay all of Chicago and all of Manila, the two cities they'd chosen for the sampling. And they must have felt much like a little child taken to F. A. O. Schwarz and told to select any toy he wished from the hundreds of thousands on display.

Which toilets to choose? Oh, the agony of it. Nothing but decisions, decisions, decisions! What if they passed up a really marvelous and exciting toilet, and wound up with nothing but some disappointing and inferior crappers?

Well, unfortunately, nobody has made a survey, nobody has rated the toilets on a graffiti basis—four stars for really hot, sizzling stuff; three stars for the more pedestrian but relatively valuable inscriptions; two stars for grades B and C stuff, and one star, or maybe no star at all, for the oft-repeated and worn-out writing. And so, the young adventurers had to set forth bravely and plunge into just any old toilet, willy-nilly.

They had their troubles. For instance, they ran into quite a few toilets that were pure and pristine, with no graffiti on the walls. And that was most exasperating, as well as a waste of precious time. And some of the toilets that did have graffiti were just dull, dull, dull.

In addition, there were other frustrations "owing to erasures, illegible writing, overlapping inscriptions, hard-leaded pencils, and the like." If there's anything meaner than a graffiti-writer who uses a hard-leaded pencil—which leaves words that are scarcely visible—I don't know what it is!

There also was the problem of how to code the various inscriptions into the proper categories, and that took plenty of time and study. The researchers finally decided to code each inscription into one category only, depending on what seemed to be the most important sense of the inscription.

For instance, the team decided to code all the "F——LBJ" inscriptions they found under the political category, rather than sex or hostility, even though either of those categories might have been good possibilities.

But the two researchers had even greater troubles. Here's how they detailed one of the problems in their report:

"Like most field studies, the present one had its hazards. First, not everyone understands why someone is loitering in toilets copying down names, phone numbers, drawings (of male and female sex organs), and things of that nature.

"One may protest that it is for science, but the stares of disbelief or the knowing leers are intimidating. And some persons are sufficiently hostile to such a brand of science as to order researchers, quite summarily, off the premises."

Another problem came from the fact that new kinds of wall coverings have been produced which either make it almost impossible to write anything legible on a wall in the first place, or which make it very easy for a custodian to remove the writing with a swish of a sponge.

Both Sechrest and Flores, rather sadly, note that many magnificent examples of graffiti have been lost because of wall coverings that resist writing, because of powerful new cleaners in the hands of unsympathetic janitors, and because of thick new layers of paint that have obliterated them forever.

"And so," they say, "we urge that those interested in exotic erotica such as graffiti begin to work in the field right away, because these developments are jeopardizing the future of such research."

eleven

TWO OTHER DISTINGUISHED RESEARCHERS INTO THE WON-
derful world of graffiti didn't have as much difficulty as
did the Sechrest team, but they did have their moments.

These researchers were Harvey D. Lomas, M.D., of the
Neuropsychiatric Institute of the University of California,
and Gershon Weltman, Ph.D., assistant professor of en-
gineering at the Biotechnology Laboratory, University of
California, both at Los Angeles.

They turned out a paper called: "What the Walls Say
Today: A Study of Contemporary Graffiti." And in it they
tell how they made forays into areas in the Los Angeles
metropolitan area equipped with camera and notepad.

At the outset, their request to collect messages written
on walls in city schools was refused by administrative offi-
cials. (Dogs in the manger, no doubt!) But Drs. Lomas and
Weltman managed to get into other public toilets all over
the city and into toilets on the university campus.

They found, among many other things, two things that
particularly interested me. One was that writing on outdoor
walls was virtually absent in middle- and upper-class com-
munities, except, as they put it, "in places where adolescents found refuge from adults." And the other was that
"the wall writer temporarily claims ownership of the wall
he embellishes."

"While photographing a wall located in a typical middle-
class community," the authors say in their paper, "we were

96

confronted by a curious youth who remarked: 'I noticed you were taking pictures of *our* wall.' "

Drs. Lomas and Weltman, unlike some researchers, who stick primarily to the toilet track, explored the great outdoors and they discovered that wherever the graffiti writer is assured of an audience—that is where he writes!

They found graffiti on bridges and freeway overpasses, alleyways, parking lots, tunnels, subways, trains, buses, trolleys, beaches, playgrounds, building walls, construction fences, electric light and telephone poles, vending machines, telephone booths, birch trees, garages, cars, trucks, and billboards—in addition, of course, to washroom walls and elevators, stairs and halls.

Noting that Freud utilized graffiti, in his study of wit and humor, as data in support of his theories of the unconscious, Drs. Lomas and Weltman found, as did Kinsey, that the graffiti in ladies' rooms were "sparse and unimaginative."

Although the Lomas-Weltman report does not go into the reason for this, it is interesting to note that Kinsey, in reporting that relatively few women write on toilet walls, declared:

"In view of our data showing that most females are not erotically aroused by the psychologic stimuli that are of significance to the male, and in view of the data showing that most females are not erotically aroused by observing sexual action, by portrayals of sexual action, or by fantasies about sexual action, there seems little doubt that the average female's lack of interest in making wall inscriptions must depend primarily upon the fact that they mean little or nothing to her erotically."

And Sechrest and Flores got pretty sick and tired of trying to find data in ladies' rooms.

"Females," they wrote, "are, in this low artistic medium, as little productive as they have long been noted to be in the higher forms such as music, literature, and painting.

"Therefore, collecting data from female conveniences is

wearing and frustrating. Some of the most likely looking places prove totally barren. Thus far we have relied upon female associates to collect inscriptions for us, but many of them have little heart for the task. As Kinsey has noted, women have little interest in pornography or other sexual stimulants. Hopefully, however, there will be, one day, an additional paper in this series which will be devoted to female graffiti."

While I understand what these learned men are getting at, and while I agree with it to some extent, I must submit that they have missed the main point.

I know why women don't write on walls as much as men. It's a very simple thing. It's merely because women, as with umbrellas, compacts, lipstick, and gloves, are always losing their pens and pencils and thus have nothing to write with when the urge seizes them.

True, they do scribble on the walls with lipstick, but this is a costly operation because any graffito longer than a word or two might well wear the lipstick down to the point of uselessness. And, as you can imagine, it would leave the lady bereft of her lipstick for the rest of the day or night—a fate not to be countenanced!

Drs. Lomas and Weltman declare that writing on walls has been a preoccupation of man from the earliest times. "The roots of wall writing arose prior to the development of language when men captured their experience by means of pictographs on cave walls. Soon symbols, then written language appeared.

"We know from Lindsay's study of Pompeii that the Romans covered their walls with diverse messages ranging from news of the day to poetic insults, concerning one another's masculinity. It is interesting that we can match messages found on the walls of Pompeii with those on the walls of Los Angeles."

The authors, in this connection, present a chart showing the similarities:

MESSAGE TYPE	POMPEII, A.D. 79	LOS ANGELES, A.D. 1965
Political Advertisement	Hermes Recommends Calventius as Mayor	Edelman for Council
Sexual Solicitation	I am yours for 2 coppers	Marion $25
The Writer and His Culture	Once a man drinks, thereafter every thing is in confusion	As far as drinking goes just have one drink, and then wait an hour (signed) A Drunk
Poetic Humor	O wall, so many men come here to scrawl, I wonder that your burdened sides don't fall	Some come here to sit & think, Others come to s—— and stink. But he must be a real screwball whose ambition is to write on a s——house wall

Professor Dundes, who also noted that the age-old inscriptions were not much different from the modern, found a sardonic scribble to support his contention. It was on the wall of The Florentine, a now-defunct Berkeley coffee house:

People probably chipped these same
things on the walls of Egyptian
bathrooms 2000 years ago
So——progress is:
A ball point pen!

Speaking of ball point pens, it might be appropriate here to tell you what Drs. Lomas and Weltman have to say about the modern methods of heralding one's thoughts.

"While the authors expected to find abundant micro-writing, i.e., writing by pen and pencil," they state, "they were surprised (and somewhat gratified) to find that these implements had been replaced outdoors by the highly visible paint-spray can, and indoors by the felt-tip marking pencil."

The outdoor writing, the authors declare, was larger, more colorful, stylized, and had a tendency to exhibit less attention to detail.

"Outdoor wall writing tended to be exhibitionist as evidenced by the abundant use of the paint-spray can in open public places. Here the adolescent defiantly marks out his pride in belonging to a group (Maynard de la Avengers), his striving for adult (authoritarian) omni-potence (Surfers Rule Supreme), his anti-social feelings by writing such things as F—— You, or embellishing the walls with swastikas and the newly popular Maltese cross.

"Erikson suggests 'Adolescence is the age of the final establishment of a dominant positive ego identity.' The walls reflect adolescent concern with group identification and the development and maintenance of a separate but imitative subculture manifested by an in-group code of symbols and sayings."

The writers declare that there is something magical

about writing on bathroom walls. "It is here, in privacy," they say, "all men seek a moment of relief and are relieved to find that they are not the only ones who have perverse ideas or homosexual fantasies. It must be reassuring, indeed, to learn that one is not alone in possession of 'dirty thoughts.'"

The authors declare that the location of pornographic or erotic graffiti "is an additional index of the manner in which the culture exerts its influence."

"In our culture," they say, "overt sexual writings occur in the more secluded locations. This may explain the increasing trends toward explicit homosexual solicitations commonly found in bathrooms, even those under middle-class influence. Here one utters the unutterable, sees the unseeable in seclusion from an ostensibly 'open' society."

This reminds me of a story that a friend of mine told me—a big, husky, thoroughly masculine guy with whom I used to play professional football.

"I went into this dump in the Village one night," he told me, "and, after a few beers, I went into the men's room. There on the wall, right over the urinal, in pretty big letters it said: 'For fun and games, call Sally.'

"And there was a telephone number. Well, having nothing to do, I thought I'd see what Sally was like and so I went to the booth and I dialed the number. There was a buzzing for a moment, and then some guy with a voice like a basso profundo answers and says: 'Hullo . . . waddya want?'

"Well, I didn't expect to get a *guy* on the phone, and I'm worried that maybe this is her husband or boy friend, and so I say, very hesitantly, 'Ah . . . well . . . is . . . ah . . . Sally there?'

"And the guy, in the deepest voice I ever heard, says: 'Yeah, *this* is Sally. Ya wanta come over?'"

Drs. Lomas and Weltman feel that all arousing or erotic messages on toilet walls are in a sense homosexual because, of course, they never were intended for a mixed audience. These messages and solicitations, as you can see, aren't written to titillate milady. Oh, no. They're just hearty, straight-from-the-shoulder, man-to-man missives. Gives a fellow a good feeling, doesn't it?

The authors indicate, by the way, that no matter how *heterosexual* the bathroom message might be, it's gotta have that fairy overtone or else it wouldn't be worth writing for an audience of males. Even pictographs of heterosexual relations, the doctors say, always show the typical homosexual concern for a *very large* dingle-berry.

Both doctors feel that wall writing is not only a universal of human behavior, but they think it's probably the lowest common denominator of communication and expression, and they state quite strongly that we haven't even begun to study it the way we should. They feel extensive surveys should be made.

Meanwhile, they say, they have to laugh about how archaeologists of the future will reconstruct our society if they base their conclusions only on our current graffiti!

twelve

INTEREST IN THE WRITING OF GRAFFITI HAS BECOME SO WIDE-spread and so intense in recent years that many restaurants, bars, dance halls, and amusement parks have put up blackboards in their toilets so people can write on them and not deface the walls.

This hasn't worked out too well. In 99 per cent of the places people steal the chalk. And in about 10 per cent of the places, they steal the blackboards, too.

Many people, however, do indeed scrawl on the blackboards, but, the owners of the places ruefully tell me, ten times as many still write on the walls, ignoring the blackboards entirely.

Another indication of graffiti's popularity is that the owners and managers of various restaurants and bars purposely put clever graffiti on their walls, whether to encourage other graffiti writers or whether merely to please the customers, I don't know.

Herb McCarthy's big restaurant in Southampton, Long Island, for instance, has two black-enameled toilet seats screwed to the wall just above the urinals. Each seat has a mirror behind it. On one seat is lettered: BE IT EVER SO HUMBLE and on the other seat are the words: THERE'S NO FACE LIKE YOUR OWN.

Then near the exit, there is painted on the wall:

Of All My Wife's Relations, I Like Sex the Best

Still another indication of how graffiti delight people is the fact that the Madison Avenue boys have embraced the idea and, in at least three or four cases, they've purposely designed ads with lots of white space so people can scrawl to their little fingers' desire. One beer company puts out a display poster that pushes its frothy product on one side and leaves the other half blank. Whether it increased beer sales, nobody knows.

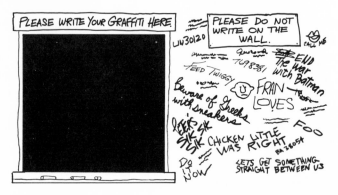

Time magazine, incidentally, held a "Group Graffiti Contest" once and invited advertising men to cleverly mark up some of the magazine's display posters, which were sent to them in the mail.

Some of the graffiti turned in were:

Marshal McLuhan Reads Books

Collier's LIVES

The Jolly Green Giant Is a Vegetable

Jerry Fields Saves [Jerry runs an advertising placement firm]

Ad Hoc Committee to Save Lord & Thomas

George Washington Hill Please Call Barney
Gallagher

$99\frac{44}{100}\%$ Is Really $99\frac{11}{25}\%$

Andy Warhol Traces

Pall Mall Can't Spall

Aunt Jemima Is an Uncle Tom

Drink Canada Dry. Visit Expo '67

I Dreamed I Could Wear a Maidenform
Bra—Twiggy

Even the staid and most respectable Players Club on Gramercy Park in Manhattan has succumbed to the urge to titillate visitors in its restrooms. And, as befitting an actors' club, the graffiti come straight out of Shakespeare. In the men's room, a neatly lettered sign reads:

Nature Her Custom Holds, Let Shame Say
What It Will

The More Haste the Less Speed

(Every once in a while some member erases the S on "Speed")
And in the ladies' room is this:

It Droppeth as the Gentle Rain from Heaven

The New Yorker magazine, as I've said, regularly runs graffiti, along with cartoons. And one of my favorites is:

Mrs. Moynihan Eats Watercress

Prisoners, by the way, are great graffiti writers. And here are some of the things they've put on the walls of late:

Dial Nine for the Bell Captain

I Am Innocent; the Warden Is Guilty

Polo Game Canceled Because of Rain

Big Pot Party Tonight—Lucky's Cell

Up the Judge!

All Screws Are Queer

Under which was written:

Ain't We Lucky?

In a restaurant near a fashionable girls' school these inscriptions somehow got into the men's room:

Boys Wanted: No Experience Necessary. Make Dates Through Millie. TL 2-0000. We're Hotter Than You Think

Hey, Guys, Don't Bother to Make Pantie Raids This Year. Nobody Wears Them (signed) Sue Ann

Are ALL *Men Homos?*

Don't TALK *About Love. Show Me!*

On Bourbon Street in New Orleans there's a brothel

across the street from a chapel. A sign on the front of the chapel declares:

Come In—We Will Lift Your Faith

On the white wall of the brothel somebody wrote:

Come In HERE*—We'll Lift More Than Your Faith*

Art Linkletter tells me that there's a sign on the front of a little Baptist church near his house in Beverly Hills that reads:

If You're Tired of Sin, Come In

Under which was written in a female hand:

If You Ain't, Call Freda CL 3-0000

Al and Pop Rissetto, owners of Lucca's Restaurant on Forty-fourth Street, Manhattan, got tired of the scribbles on their lavatory walls and had them painted over one day. That very night somebody got even by writing:

The Painter's Work Has Been in Vain
The Phantom Writer Strikes Again

Another restaurateur put up a sign:

Please Keep This Washroom Clean

To which someone appended:

Yeah. Piss in the Dining Room

Two graffiti are unusual and most intriguing. One of them, written on the side of a building about four inches above the sidewalk, reads:

Will I Ever Grow Up?

And the other, written way down on the baseboard in a men's room, says:

I'm Feelin' Mighty Low Today

Some other washroom graffiti include:

Shout hip hip and jump for joy
I was here before Kilroy

What Do You Do Till the Call Girl Comes?

Twiggy Is Bottomless

(In a choked toilet): *The Plumber is* NOT
dead—But He Might Just As Well Be

108

Captain Kangaroo Tells Dirty Jokes to Grandmothers

Promise Her Anything but Give Her LSD

George Schleppington Washed Here

Do Not Stand While the Room Is in Motion

Do Not Leave Toilet While Bowels Are in Motion

Enovid Is for My Id

Syphilis Can Be Fun

(In a ladies room) : *If you're Going More Often and Enjoying*
It Less, Try the Men's Room

Don't Be a Star—Use Both Hands

The World is a F—— Sandwich, and Every Day We Take a Bite of It

Is There Life After Birth?

Evil-Eye Fleagle Is a Fag

TWIGGY IS BOTTOMLESS

Copulate for Co-Existence

LSD—Better Living Through Chemistry

LSD Means Liberty Syka-Delic

Wombmate Wanted

A Merry Christmas to All Our Readers

More Deviation—Less Population

Absinthe Makes the Heart Grow Fonder

To Go Together Is Blessed; To Come To-gether Divine

Peter Pan Is Alive and Well in Greenwich Village

To which was added:

Would You Believe with Tinkerbelle?

Here's a sampling of what's being written on walls in phone booths:

Clark Kent Is a Transvestite

Send a Get-Well Card to LBJ

Whoever Reads This—I Love You!

No Easter This Year—They Found the Body

John Birch Is Politically Disoriented

Roses are reddish
Violets are bluish
If it weren't for Xmas
We'd all be Jewish

Keep the Pope off the Moon

Neurosis is Red
Melancholia is Blue
I'm Schizophrenic
What Are You?

110

*I Think I'm a Chicken. I Ain't Got Hair on
my Chest. Just Feathers*

Avoid the Christmas Rush. Drink Now

*Thanks, Dr. Coppolino, but I've Already Had
My Shots*

Dean Rusk Is a Recorded Announcement

*Fight the Computer—Bend, Fold, Staple
Crease and Mutilate Punch Cards*

Stamp Out Distemper, But Don't Step IN It

Stay Loyal to the Police State

Pussy Galore for President

Santha Rama Rau . . . Rau! Rau! Rau!

*Sorry, Charlie. I Gave Up and Went to the
Hotel*

Stop Vandalism—Don't Scribble on Walls

*In Case of Atomic Attack, the Federal Rul-
ing against Prayer in Schools Will Be Temporarily Suspended*

*'Tis the Christmas Season—Everybody Make
Mary!*

There's a residential building on Park Avenue South
near Nineteenth Street in New York City that has had a
graffiti mystery for nearly four years. One day the superintendent of the building went out on the sidewalk and
found that someone had written in huge, black letters on
on the whitish wall:

Psychiatrist Is Whore

Not "a" psychiatrist is a whore, or not that psychiatrists
are whores, but just:

111

Psychiatrist Is Whore

The lettering was done in heavy black crayon, but the super finally got it washed off. About three weeks later, he was surprised to find the inscription had been put there again:

Psychiatrist Is Whore

He washed it off and the building was clean for some three months. Then the same legend appeared again. This has been going on for nearly four years and nobody ever has seen anybody write "Psychiatrist Is Whore" but it sure as hell gets written. How and why, nobody knows.

Psychiatrists often get batted around by the wall writing. Here's an example. Somebody, using lipstick, wrote on the white stone front of a Park Avenue building:

People Are No Damned Good

Under this somebody wrote:

Psychiatrists Are Worse

And under that was written:

Psychiatrists Aren't People

There's a restaurant in Greenwich Village which has a sign outside proclaiming:

Costs Nothing to Come In

Under this some disgruntled patron wrote:

Yeah, But You Better Be Loaded to Get Out!!!

112

There's another restaurant-night club in Greenwich Village which, claiming to be a landmark, has a sign:

Aaron Burr Stabled His Horses Here

And a patron added:

Sure Smells Like It

In Luigi's Restaurant, 19 Murray Street, New York City, the boss-man, Louis Dossena, put up a sign in the men's room reading:

Employees Must Wash Hands Before Leaving This Room

To which a nettled employee added:

Better That Management Should

It was at Luigi's incidentally, that I first saw the graffito:

Judge Crater—Call Your Office

On the sidewalk in front of the all-glass Lever House on Park Avenue, Manhattan, somebody scrawled:

In Case of Emergency, Break Glass and Pull Lever Down

And even in Viet Nam there's a rash of graffiti. One big hand-lettered sign proclaims:

Welcome Marines—The Road That Got You Here Was Built by the Seabees

113

Signs on tents include:

George Washington Never Slept Here, but Pvt. Purdy Does

The Hanoi Hilton

It Don't Look Like Much, But It's Home

On the roof of one small house is painted:

Chew Mail Pouch Tobacco

And next to that is painted:

See Rock City

Over a door through which generals go is painted: "Private Mess," and over the door through which privates go is painted: "General Mess."

My favorite is the graffito scrawled on the side of a 155mm. howitzer. It reads:

Herman's Howitzer—We Get a Bang Out of Our Job

But I guess the champion graffito of them all is the one that Professor Allen Walker Read found in the men's room of Shady Camp, near Brady, Nebraska, when he visited there on August 24, 1928. Crudely lettered it read:

I have a girl in Indiana
She like to play with my banana
She can sing and she can dance
And she has whiskers in her pants

So—now you know what that anthropoid ape started back in 1,000,000 B.C. when he decided to become a Pithecanthropus erectus and scribbled on the wall:

Joe Loves Dottie

Where will it all end? Nobody knows. We'll just have to watch the handwriting on the walls—truly the scrawl of the wild!